ANNEXE DE LA BIBLIOTHEQUE
uOttawa
LIBRARY ANNEX

International Business-Government Affairs: Toward an Era of Accommodation

International Business-Government Affairs

Toward an Era of Accommodation

Edited by
John Fayerweather
New York University

Ballinger Publishing Company • Cambridge, Mass.
A Subsidiary of J.B. Lippincott Company

Library of Congress Catalog Card Number: 73-12445

International Standard Book Number: 0-88410-256-4

Printed in the United States of America

Library of Congress Cataloging in Publication Data

Workshop in International Business-Government Affairs,
New York University, 1972.
The government and the multinational firm.

Background papers prepared for the workshop, as well as a summary of the discussions.
1. International business enterprises-Congresses.
2. Industry and state-Congresses. I. Title.
HD69.I7W63 338.8'8 73-12445
ISBN 0-88410-256-4

Contents

Foreword

There is growing awareness throughout the world of the common interest of government and business in trade affairs. There is an equal awareness of the potential for conflict that failure of understanding between these two parties could generate. The opportunity for the academic world to observe the government-business interrelationships and to extrapolate from what they see is a great one. Yet, the danger is that observations may be made and conclusions drawn without full understanding of the motivations of either of the active parties.

The seminar on which this book is based is a very real attempt to overcome the risks of romanticizing the conflict rather than documenting the opportunities for cooperation. Much credit is due the members of the New York University Graduate School of Business who saw the need for open dialogue. All of us who participated certainly gained a better understanding of the views of others and found a much more common sense of interest than I, for one, would have anticipated.

To be sure, there was disagreement among the participants and some still remains. I, for example, believe that the years since the end of World War II have been much more an era of accommodation than one of confrontation as it is sometimes characterized. Even so, the dominant theme of the conference and of this book lies in the element of common interest rather than confrontation. I am confident that if more dialogues of this type take place, then the resolution of conflicting objectives is more likely to come about in a way which will be constructive for government and business alike. Ultimately the consumer everywhere would benefit most.

E. S. Groo

New York

Preface

The Workshop in International Business-Government Affairs was the sixth in a program of workshops in international business, conducted by the Graduate School of Business Administration of New York University. The program was initiated in 1964 with the support of a grant from the Ford Foundation, and continued in subsequent years with support from a number of sponsoring business firms, as a means to foster education and research in international business.

The first four workshops organized by Professor Fayerweather were designed to help business schools develop programs of study in international business. Some eighty-five professors, each with a major responsibility for a school's international courses, participated in these programs. The workshops dealt with the full range of international business subjects by means of seminar discussions and extensive field interviews in the large New York international business community, and the cooperation of many executives. This set of workshops contributed to the rapid process of establishment of new international programs conducted by business schools throughout the country in the mid-1960s.

By the end of the 1960s it was apparent that the major need for helping other schools to start international studies had been accomplished. At the same time, a new need had emerged in terms of the increasing number of people doing research in the field, and the major subjects calling for research attention. The workshop program was, therefore, redirected to focus on specific subjects, and the format was changed to bring together a limited number of people with strong competence in the various subjects. In 1970, sixteen leading academicians assembled for the first of these workshops, which dealt with Comparative Management under Professor Boddewyn's direction.

The choice of International Business-Government Affairs for the second specialized workshop stemmed from the critical importance of the subject and the special interest of the NYU business faculty—three of its members (Professors Boddewyn, Fayerweather and Kapoor) being engaged in interrelated research work in the area. To discuss the subject effectively, it was clear that we would need not only leading academic researchers, but also practitioners from both business and government, and inputs of viewpoints from various countries. The resultant group of eighteen participants, listed on page xv, included four executives from multinational firms, three former or present members of foreign governments (two of whom also had had considerable business experience), two former senior U. S. government officials, as well as six foreign and five U. S. academicians. The latter included men from the fields of economics, law, sociology, and political science, as well as business school professors. Every continent was represented, except Africa. As a consequence, the group could draw upon all types of competence relevant to analysis of the problems of international business-government affairs.

The workshop discussions were clearly of greatest value to those who participated. However, the intent of the workshop program being to serve a broader public, we have attempted to pass on as much of the content as possible in published form. Previous workshops have already resulted in two books [published by New York University, Graduate School of Business Administration: *International Business Education: Curriculum Planning,* by John Fayerweather, J. Boddewyn, and Holger Engberg (1966); and *Comparative Management: Teaching, Training and Research,* edited by J. Boddewyn (1970), the latter having been distributed by New York University Press]. The present book follows this policy by presenting the background papers prepared for the workshop as well as the results of the discussion.

The workshop would not have been possible without the generous financial help of our sponsors listed on page xiii. We are most appreciative of the strong support of these firms, many of whom have backed the workshop program from its outset, and some of whom we welcomed to the program for the first time. Our other great debt is to the participants in the workshop, whose intellectual contributions were the heart of our accomplishments.

I also wish to record a special note of appreciation to J. Roy Galloway and Todd Groo, who advised me regularly on the plans for the workshop. It was regrettable, but characteristic of our group, that Mr. Galloway (and some other expected participants) were called away suddenly by international corporate responsibilities, and thus were unable to join in the discussion.

At the operational level, we are indebted to Richard Spivak, whose efficiency as administrative assistant made the workshop run smoothly and effectively, and to the workshop secretary, Della Pruitt, whose diligent handling of the correspondence and manuscripts was a vital component of the process.

John Fayerweather

New York

The Workshop Sponsors

The corporations and foundations whose contributions financed the Workshop in International Business-Government Affairs

American Metal Climax Foundation
Bechtel Corporation
Caterpillar Tractor Company
Chase Manhattan Bank
General Electric Company
First National City Bank
IBM World Trade Corporation
International Telephone and Telegraph Corporation
Insular Lumber Company
Merck, Sharp and Dohme International
Standard Oil Company (New Jersey)
Union Carbide Corporation
Westinghouse Electric Corporation

Workshop Participants

Professor Jack N. Behrman, Graduate School of Business Administration, North Carolina University and former U. S. Assistant Secretary of Commerce.

Professor David Blake, Graduate Schools of Business and Department of Political Science, University of Pittsburg.

Professor J. Boddewyn, Baruch College, City University of New York.

S. Boothalingham, Director General, National Council of Applied Economic Research; former Secretary, Ministry of Finance, India

Professor Michel Crozier, Senior Research Director, Centre National de la Recherche Scientifique and Director, Centre de Sociologie des Organisations, Paris, France.

Professor John Fayerweather, Graduate School of Business Administration, New York University.

Olivier Giscard d'Estaing, Deputy, National Assembly and former Director, Institut European d'Administration des Affairs, (INSEAD), France.

J. F. E. Gillespie, Legal Advisor, Union Carbide Eastern.

Elmer S. Groo, Vice President, IBM World Trade Corporation.

Professor Ashok Kapoor, Graduate School of Business Administration, New York University.

Professor Eric W. I. Kierans, Member of Parliament and Faculty of Management, McGill University, former Minister of Canadian Department of Communications.

Professor Noritake Kobayashi, Keio University, Tokyo, Japan.

Dr. Mario Leserna Pinson, Former Rector, Universidad de los Andes.

Professor Isaiah Allan Litvak, School of International Affairs, Carleton University, Ottawa, Canada.

Professor J. Alex Murray, Faculty of Business Administration and Director of the Seminar on Canadian-American Relations, University of Windsor.

Professor Richard D. Robinson, School of Management, Massachusetts Institute of Technology and Lecturer, Department of History Harvard University.

Jerome M. Rosow, Manager, Planning Division, Public Affairs Department, Standard Oil Company (New Jersey) and former Assistant Secretary of Labor for Policy, Evaluation and Research.

Henry S. Thompson, President, Insular Lumber Company

International Business-Government Affairs: Toward an Era of Accommodation

Chapter One

Introduction

TOWARD THE ERA OF ACCOMMODATION

The quarter century since World War II can aptly be labeled as the "era of confrontation" between the nation state and the multinational firm. Hopefully the next quarter century will be the "era of accommodation" between these great institutions.

Within the era of confrontation, the multinational firms moved into areas of economic opportunity at an explosive rate; U. S. direct investment, for example, expanded over sixfold from $12 billion in 1945 to $78 billion in 1970. Offering important contributions from their great resources of capital and skills, the firms were valued as participants in the economic development so urgently sought throughout the world.

But limited prior experience with international companies had not prepared society for such a massive institutional change. Consequently, both firms and nations were catapulted into largely unexplored and undeveloped political territory. As the activities of the former grew, their implications for a wide range of national interests became a matter of prime preoccupation of governments. Economic development, military security, technological progress, cultural identity, and other vital concerns were now substantially guided or, at least, heavily influenced by the multinational firms. Because of the momentum of the expansion and undeveloped political processes, the varied problems along the interface between the firms and governments essentially appeared to be a confrontation. Traumatic conflicts were not uncommon, ad hoc improvisation of conflict resolution was typical, and mutual understanding on either side was limited.

But, in an age when even the Americans and Communist Chinese have seen that they must learn to talk and live together, responsible leaders have come to recognize that accommodation must supercede confrontation. Some were already exploring that direction some years ago. By the mid-fifties a few people were scouting the still-elusive idea of a mutual code of investment conduct to guide investors and governments. In 1957, the Business Council for International Understanding undertook a pioneering effort in which leaders of the Indian government and multinational firms worked out a document of joint understanding of objectives and issues. As is always true of sociopolitical experimentation, these efforts moved slowly—some failing, some sputtering, and some inching along.

In the early 1970s, however, one could sense that the accommodation process was starting to make significant progress. Traumatic confrontations still occurred—such as the Chilean expropriations of 1971—but negotiation had become the standard process along the international business-government interface. Negotiations could be immensely difficult; the engagements between the Organization of Petroleum Exporting Countries (OPEC) and the petroleum firms being a prime example. Still, the pace and tenor on both sides in most situations indicated a more moderate and balanced assessment of problems and practical resolution. Perhaps the most arresting illustration of the transition that has been accomplished is the Mexican case. The dramatic expropriations of the oil properties in 1938 were forerunners of the general pattern of the era of confrontation. By 1972, however, Mexico was managing a process of progressive Mexicanization which, while not welcomed by multinational firms, was so judiciously handled that the pace of expansion of the firms in Mexico was unabated.

These signs of progress are heartening to those who believe that the tremendous problems of the world require the best joint efforts of national governments and multinational firms. But, they are just a start on a long road to fully effective accommodation. There is a vast lack of understanding, and misunderstanding, on both sides, aggravated by mistrust and nationalistic biases. We are still a long way from knowing which interests and objectives of governments and firms will best serve the welfare of the people of the world—knowledge which should provide the guiding criteria in decision making. We are at a very early stage in experimentation with institutional arrangements for productive endeavors and for the resolution of differences.

This is the context of the Workshop in International Business-Government Affairs. To a man, the assembled group of academic, business, and government participants believed profoundly in the desirability and feasibility of accommodation. Optimistically believing that the era of confrontation was passing, we could look back to its troubled times for experience from which to draw wisdom. We were acutely conscious of the multitude of questions which would have to be dealt with before accommodation could be said to be the established norm for international business-government affairs. Our deliberations were directed squarely to defining these questions and suggesting avenues of approach which would be useful as guides for the practitioners of business and government, and the researchers of academia. The substantial range of agreement which developed in our discussions was, in itself, an encouraging sign that the era of accommodation was gathering momentum.

THE WORKSHOP BOOK

This book presents seven papers, written by participants to serve as background for the workshop subject, and a concluding chapter which summarizes the workshop discussion.

The papers deal with selected areas of international business-government affairs. There is no presumption that they cover the subject area completely. The problems of international business-government interaction are too broad to attempt that type of coverage here. Rather, our approach was to identify what we felt were particularly significant aspects of the subject. The primary goal of the workshop was to provide guidance for future research in the field. Thus the topics of the papers were selected, in part, according to our judgement of the areas in which fruitful work can be done. Each paper outlines the main dimensions of the topic and directions for future research.

The papers have been arranged roughly in a sequence running from environmental factors through policy and organization, to operating processes, though there is substantial intermingling of content among papers according to that sort of classification. John Fayerweather's chapter deals particularly with the attitudes within host nations, which are major influences upon the positions of governments. Richard Robinson examines the broad structural characteristics of multinational firms in the context of nation-state goals and pressures. Jack Behrman focuses on a single major issue of world economic evolution—the integration of industrial production—and the ways in which governments and multinational firms may interact to handle it. Richard Robinson's second paper focuses on a second concrete interaction area—the establishment of entry terms when new investments are made—in which the interaction of business and government goals comes into its sharpest definition. J. Boddewyn examines the organizational implications of the international business-government interaction in its evolving form—the external affairs function of the multinational firm. David Blake's chapter looks both broadly and in specific terms at the very sensitive issue of the role of the multinational firm in its relation to the political process of host nations. Ashok Kapoor completes the set with a discussion of the level of highly concrete interaction of business and government—the negotiation process—at which the attitudes, goals, policies, and organizational systems converge in efforts to reach accommodation on specific issues.

Chapter Two

Attitudes Affecting International Business-Government Affairs

John Fayerweather

Attitudes play a significant part in international business-government affairs. There is little question as to the validity of that assertion. It is generally acknowledged, not only by behavioral scientists, but also by the economists who have done major portions of the research on international business-government relations (e. g., Behrman, Mikesell and Vernon).[1]

But despite this acceptance of the importance of attitudes there has been little progress in study of them. The common present thinking on the subject is well stated by Vernon, "In sum, the existing level of tension generated by U. S.-controlled subsidiaries in host countries cannot be explained merely in terms of conflicts of economic interests. . . . In search of prime causes one is pushed off economics into the political, social and cultural variables. Variables of this sort, of course, are difficult to distinguish and difficult to measure. The viscera prove more important than the cerebrum as the instrument of analysis".[2]

While the viscera will undoubtedly continue to be an important source of insights, the intent of this paper is to examine more scientific routes to study of the relevant attitudes. Before discussing a strategy for research, however, it is necessary to define the territory to be explored.

What Attitudes?

The definitional process must start at the bottom with the meaning of "attitudes." It is convenient to imply a dichotomous distinction in which attitudes are considered emotional, nonrational reactions as distinguished from rational considerations related to tangible interests. There is utility in this distinction but it is an oversimplification. The emotional responses of an individual in a given situation, which are commonly described as attitudes, are those which cannot be related readily to the rational analysis of the matter at hand along tangible lines of economic interests, military security, etc. But they may be rooted either in tangible past experience or expectation of effects upon specific interests in the future. Furthermore, there is a blending of the emotional and the rational in the mind of the individual which defies simple dichotomous separation. A further complication arises when we attempt to define types of attitudes because we are, in fact, dealing with an emotional-rational process which has a unique composite of origins for each person, and which is only partially susceptible to classification systems constructed by social scientists.

These complications cannot be allowed to obstruct research but they are an essential starting point for planning research. Research will be most efficient if it proceeds both from established bodies of knowledge and methodologies, and in delimited conceptual frameworks. But uncertain definition of the territory suggests a constant need for recognition of the tentative character of such approaches. A useful example here is the transition in the study of nationalism over the past forty years, which originally was the province of political science, but is now seen to be as much, if not more, susceptible to the techniques of social psychologists. Thus, any present prescription for research on attitudes in this area can only be one's best judgment of what is useful at this moment, probably to be revised substantially in a few years.

With this caveat in mind, the selection of research strategy must start by defining the relevant attitudes so far as is practical on the basis of existing knowledge. The definition of "attitudes" in this discussion will remain imprecise and will rest, essentially, upon specifics of the kinds of personal attributes which are identified as present and requiring study. In this approach to defining the territory two classification frameworks are useful: functionally-related attitudes and scientific fields.

The concept of functionally-related attitudes seems useful because it provides a basis for limiting research attention in a territory which offers a very broad range of possible subjects. On the basis of general knowledge, supported by the limited research available (notably that of Behrman),[3] we can identify four main functional aspects of host nations in which attitudes evoked by the activities of foreign firms appear significant: loss of control of national affairs, dependence, economic results, and cultural impact.

1. Fear of loss of control of national affairs arises mainly from two aspects of multinational firm activities. First, the extent to which the parent organization makes decisions affecting host-nation operations and second, the degree of power which the firm can command, giving it a different status with respect to host government economic control measures, as opposed to strictly domestic firms, e. g. better access to credit. There are tangible effects from both of these sources which enter into the rational analysis of national interest, but beyond them there are attitudinal resistances to loss of control which will be elaborated upon below.
2. Dependence, especially in scientific technology, carries definite economic and military security costs, but beyond them it stimulates certain emotions which properly fall in the area of attitudes.
3. Attitudes toward economic results logically should be entirely in the area

of rational analysis. In fact, however, research indicates that attitudes along nonrational lines are significant (Fayerweather and McMillan)[4] because of inadequacies of economic analytical approaches and the strength of certain attitudes bearing on the subject, notably nationalistic instincts to protect host-nation wealth, and to suspect predatory intents of outside entities penetrating the home society.

4. The cultural impact commonly perceived as the "Americanization" of host societies falls naturally in the attitudinal area because cultural values and satisfactions are so intimately associated with attitudes.

Present knowledge provides a tentative basis for distinguishing between these functional subjects as a guide to future research. My studies of elite attitudes in Britain, Canada, and France indicate that the control aspect is the most critical element, with the economic attitudes positioned a little lower on the scale, though still quite important.[5] The cultural aspect seems distinctly less significant. The elites rated it lower in importance, and generally expressed favorable views of the cultural impact of foreign firms. Thus, it does not seem fruitful to devote substantial effort to research of it. The surveys did not include questions about dependence. However, other research (Behrman)[6] suggests that it falls somewhere within the range of importance of the control and economic aspects. Comparable surveys have not been made in less developed countries, but modest explorations with similar questionnaires given to Korean and Philippine students indicate that the pattern is similar. Furthermore, general indications drawn from such developments as the Andean Pact and evolution of Indian foreign investment policy suggest that the control and economic attitudes are the dominant factors.

A determination of the relative significance of control vs. economic attitudes is not entirely necessary, because pursuit of both will be important. However, given limited research capabilities, some weighting is useful. While present knowledge provides some guidelines on this point, a few words from one individual seem equally instructive. In a conversation with the author in 1970 Senator Diokno of the Philippines, a leader in the nationalistic movement against multinational firms, expressed his philosophy in a capsule: "If we can establish our control over the foreign firms, we can then take care of economic and other problems without difficulty." With this as an indication of the functional area which may be expected to receive the highest priority by host governments, it seems logical to concentrate on the control attitudes.

While classification by functional fields provides some useful guidance in setting priorities for research, the behavioral science classification is useful in defining relevant concepts and methodologies. If our focus is on control of national affairs, it appears that useful consideration of attitudes may be related to three behavioral science subjects: nationalism, social role, and political-economic ideology.

Nationalistic attitudes are central to international business-government affairs, because they are, by definition, present in internation relations. I have developed quite fully elsewhere the conceptual relation of nationalism and the multinational firm.[7] It will suffice here to emphasize the central role of control of national affairs in nationalism. The adherence by members of a society to their nation is intimately associated with their conviction that the national structure will serve as a source of security and give them other important benefits. This belief derives from the assurance that control of the nation will be directed by their co-nationals in the interest of the national body. The multinational firm, as an outsider exercising control of national affairs, is fundamentally a challenge to this system. A basic nationalistic resistance to the multinational firm is, therefore, consistent with the concepts of nationalism.

The social role element relates to the elites, essentially. The basic proposition is that the control function of certain elites is challenged by the multinational firm. Government officials, businessmen, labor leaders, and others, have acquired both skill and power within the national system which permits them to function for themselves and for their constituents. The multinational firm disrupts this status by the capabilities and power it can exert outside the national societal framework. Thus, its activities will tend to arouse attitudinal resistances of the same general nature as are found in any control-role disruption situation. While he provides no concrete research basis, Vernon presents useful ideas along these lines.[8]

The political-economic ideological aspect is a somewhat different order of attitudinal issue, because it is not, in a conceptual sense, distinctively a foreign firm-host nation issue, as are the first two subjects. As commonly experienced, it is basically the issue of large-scale private enterprise vs. variations of socialism. Essentially the same issue exists within host nations, between dominant big business firms and leftist political sectors. However, it recurs so frequently, intimately intertwined with other attitudinal reactions toward multinational firms, that it should be included here, if only because its influence must be identified in order to properly evaluate the effects of other types of attitudes. For example, the best-selling Canadian book, *Silent Surrender,* devotes at least as much attention to inveighing against multinational firms as dictators of consumer-buying practices as against nationalism per se, even though it is commonly characterized among Canadians as an expression of the popular nationalism.[9]

These three elements provide the main conceptual base for investigating attitudes toward control of national affairs in international business-government relations. Specific development of the concepts requires further attention to which, hopefully, competent behavioral scientists will contribute. One promising development has been the work of Harold Kelman and his associates in dissecting attitudes currently grouped under the heading of nationalism.[10] They identified three sets of attitudes characteristic of the form which nationalism takes among different types of people: symbolic, normative, and functional. An interesting part of this model is the similarity of the attitudes of the functional nationalist to the elite status role concept outlined above. The affinity of the people in the functional group toward the nation is heavily weighted by the specific benefits which participation in the national system affords, including, among other things, the opportunities for advancement provided. One can reasonably project from this to the specific role and status which the national system may provide as a probable further attribute of a people's feelings toward their nation. This similarity between the nationalism and social role concepts underscores the artificiality of classifying behavioral patterns under specific headings. Such points, and the prospects for future fundamental research in social sciences, are interesting, but as they are not appropriate for immediate application to international business-government affairs, they will not be pursued further here.

Propositions Underlying Future Research

Concentrating on the functional level, I believe the territory for most fruitful research lies within specific attitudes toward control of national affairs emanating from the combination of nationalism and social roles. Political-economic ideology will inevitably appear in the midst of this research. Attitudes on dependence, wealth, and culture will also intrude as related factors, and should receive attention, though less than that given the control element. Specifically it is proposed that a research plan be followed which adds to our descriptive knowledge of attitudes and tests propositions pertinent to the behavior of both international firms and host governments.

As the propositions are central to the research plan, they will be set forth briefly here. These represent concepts based on research to date as to the character of the control issue, the nature and implications of host-national attitudes on it, and the dynamic effects of these attitudes.

The propositions start with the assumption that host nationals fall broadly into two categories, with distinctive attitude characteristics and a significant interrelation between them.

First, there is the general public which is poorly informed on the specific issues involving multinational firms, and lacks either interest or competence to understand them in appreciable depth. These people have a diffused nationalistic reaction against multinational firms, which emanates from a basic belief in the nation as the central unit for decision making and an instinct to protect its integrity and apparent interests.

Second, there are the elites (politicians, labor leaders, businessmen, intellectuals, etc.), who have to some degree the same attitudes as the general public, but are more strongly influenced by a combination of their societal role attitudes and more sophisticated knowledge and competence in the specific issues when dealing with multinational firms.

The elite and general public attitudes are tied together in a manner which is mutually reinforced by the appeal-support process. The elites make appeals for support of their institutional roles in decisions by use of nationalistic themes. These themes foster the nationalistic attitudes of the public. The appeals, and the response of the public, create pressures on the elites, which constrain them to act in ways consistent with the nationalistic themes.

Another essential assumption is that multinational firms can make real contributions to the welfare of the host nation but this requires the exercise of central control, which the host national attitudes resist. These benefits, in the main, stem from economies of global rationalization in such matters as logistics, and research and development. Where such benefits do not exist, the arguments for exercising control contrary to the desires of host nationals are weak, and, indeed, the long-term utility and viability of the multinational firm is uncertain. In any case, the research here is concerned only with the substantial range of situations in which true benefits for host nationals appear to require exercise of central control by the firm.

Three propositions proceed from these assumptions. The first is that there will be a transition in nationalistic attitudes toward acceptance of the multinational control. History records a steady shift of attitudes toward acceptance by people of control from progressively higher levels of social institutions, nationalism itself being the attitudinal expression of this acceptance of control at that level—an acceptance yet to be accomplished fully in many new nations. A similar process of acceptance of certain degrees of multinational control in business (as well as military affairs, monetary relations, etc.), can be projected. The process by which acceptance is achieved requires time and a series of successful events. Essentially, it depends upon an accumulation of experiences with multinational control which people find satisfy their own interests. These, along with institutional changes which provide adequate protection of those interests, lead to confidence in the beneficial character of multinational control. At the same time, there must be subsidence of the use of nationalistic appeals emanating from the elite.

The second proposition is that there will be certain institutional changes which, in part, absorb the control desires of host nationals. It is assumed that, where appropriate, binational or multinational control institutions will evolve to deal with activities of multinational firms in which two or more nations have an interest. The elites of host nations will participate in these institutions, transferring to them their social role attitudes. The conventional suggestions of corporations chartered under, and supervised by, the United Nations do not seem consistent with realities. It seems more likely that over the foreseeable future (20 to 30 years), the evolution will be by confederation of national level groups into units exercising multinational constraints on firms in specific decision-making areas. The emergence of OPEC and the start at multinational labor organization are suggestive of this evolution. The evolution will be slow, since it requires perception by various elites of common interests with those of counterparts in other countries, evolution away from their well-established pattern of relating their thinking and actions primarily to national reference groups, institutional forms for cooperative action, and other changes.

The third proposition is that the transitions anticipated in the first two propositions will require dynamic processes with certain characteristics:

a. The rate of transition is governed by the speed with which major social elements can change, notably (1) attitude shifts toward acceptance of multinational control, and (2) reorientation of elites from nation-oriented ways to participation in multinational control systems. Both must be slow in light of the many human interactions which tend to reinforce the established patterns. This time factor puts emphasis on (1) expediting of experiments in involvement of elites in multinational control systems, and (2) actions which buy time and divert attention from critical issues, thereby reducing the tensions which tend to reinforce existing attitudes and nation-oriented structures.

b. Since people's actions are largely governed by their horizon of expectations and perceptions, which are quite short range, the short-range action patterns of firms' behavior have a major effect. Specifically, in the current stage of evolution both the elites and general populace of host nations are strongly affected by fear of losses of control over the next few years. There is pressure, therefore, on firms either to avoid visible actions aggravating these fears, or to actually do things to lessen them. On an immediate basis there is a need to provide ongoing satisfaction of desires for control of national affairs by specific actions.

Both (a) and (b) may be beneficially affected by nation-level behavior to ease attitudinal tensions. A substantial range of actions may be taken by both firms and governments which conform to nationalistic attitudes without serious impairment of significant exercise of central multinational control—employment of top level local national executives, issuance of financial data on subsidiaries, etc. Many of these actions are sound in themselves, but in the transition process they are useful as a means of buying time and fostering good will while the critical process of achieving acceptance of multinational control of important decisions progresses.

Likewise, bilateral government actions may be taken on overlapping sovereignty issues. The problems here (antitrust, taxation, etc.) are marginal to the main issues of multinational business control. They must be resolved, however, in the interests of the long run development of an orderly environment for business. Focusing upon them, thus, does have a utilitarian function. In the transition process, their chief value would appear to be that of providing an outlet for the control objectives of some of the elites, a means for evolving their participation in a control structure higher than the nation level so their orientation might start to change, and, again, to buy time by diverting attention to a set of issues which could be readily dealt with and away from the more difficult central control issues.

In brief, the underlying proposition set forth is that when central control of business decisions is actually beneficial for economic reasons, the multinational firms will succeed in exercising that control, despite the current desire of members of nations to retain control at the national level. The initial achievement of multinational control is accomplished against broad nationalistic resistance by use of the strength residing in the firm's command of technology, the economic benefits its superior logistic system can bestow, and its other capabilities. Its performance in serving the interests of the people is tested and developed against the competition of nation-oriented business institutions and nationalistic pressures. An attitudinal transition occurs in time, along with certain institutional changes which lead to true acceptance of the control, rather than a tension-filled acceptance. This transition requires time during which performance of multinational control is observed, confidence in it is acquired, and participation of elites in multinational control institutions evolves.

Future Research

As an introduction to proposals for future research on attitudes affecting internation-business government affairs it seems wise to reemphasize the broad characterizations made at the start of the chapter. We are dealing with a poorly-defined area in which it is hard to develop effective research methodologies, and upon which limited work has been undertaken. Under these circumstances, the expectations for research over the next few years should be modest. Furthermore, one must guard against the hazard that whatever efforts are made may become lost in the morass, particularly if they attempt to break into the middle of undeveloped subject matter and methodology. Sound general strategy in such a situation would seem to require caution in moving from two reasonably solid bases: first, the fundamental behavioral science studies, and, second, empirical research with a substantial operating orientation. As noted earlier, recommendations for behavioral science research are beyond the scope of this paper. Hopefully, studies such as Kelman and his associates have made will progress steadily to provide a sounder conceptual foundation for business-oriented studies. Focusing on the latter, I suggest four areas as most fruitful for immediate attention: knowledge of the nature of attitudes, attitudinal reactions to corporate behavior, effects of the attitudes, and elite attitudes in multinational institutions.

1. Understanding the Nature of Attitudes. We know from work to date that there is substantial variety in the attitudes of individual host nationals in at least three dimensions: issues (control, culture, etc.); basic origins (nationalism, social roles, and political-economic ideology); and groups (labor leaders, businessmen, etc.). But our definition of these variations is still limited to a few broad features, such as the relatively greater concern over control vs. culture, and the more negative viewpoints of labor leaders compared to other elites in a few developed countries.[11] We do not, therefore, have the basis for predictive and analytical work which is required for immediate business application and for more advanced research study.

High priority therefore should be assigned to further analysis of the nature of the attitudes of host nationals. Two general directions are suggested for this work: First, broad survey research comparable to that already accomplished in the developed countries should be extended to the LDC's. It seems probable that some of the main variation patterns will differ there. For example, the relation between attitudes of businessmen and labor may be different from those in the advanced countries, because multinational firms have a greater competitive impact and their labor-relations situation is different from that of advanced countries.

Second, there is a need to further explore attitudes to determine more clearly their origins, both basic causes (e. g., nationalism), and possible socioeconomic origins (e. g., education, work experience, etc.). While the questionnaire-survey work done to date has been somewhat informative along these lines,[12] the complexity of the attitudes and determinants are such that depth interviewing is probably in order for the next stage of research. Such interviewing, presumably, should also lead to an improvement in the composition of questionnaires which will be more fruitful for future work.

The analysis of attitudes to increase predictive capability leads also to aggregate differences among nations. This type of analysis is closely related to the substantial amount of work which has already been done on investment climates and government attitudes by Litvak and Maule, Nehrt, Robock, Root, and others.[13] To date studies in this area have relied on macro-data; historical experience, economic conditions, etc. The incorporation of attitudinal information based on aggregations of information about individuals and groups is a useful component in the study of overall national policies towards foreign business. By the same token consideration of the other factors will provide useful insights in the analysis of aggregate differences in attitudes between nations.

To cite just one illustration of the problems and potentials for research here, I will note the interesting comparison between Britain and France and Canada. In the late 1940s, foreign companies controlled 5 percent or so of manufacturing in Britain and France, and about 45 percent in Canada. This degree of control apparently aroused no great concern in any of the countries. By 1972, the percentages had increased to nearly 10 percent in Britain and France, and 60 percent in Canada. Historical data presented by Murray indicate a considerable increase recently in national concern about foreign investment among Canadians.[14] Yet, my survey of elites also shows that worries in Canada about the critical area of control of national affairs by foreigners are only slightly greater than in Britain and France.[15] Why should attitudes have changed substantially in a period when control of foreign investment has increased by only about 30 percent from an already very high figure of 45 percent? Why should the concern among elites be only a little greater in Canada than in the European countries, when control of investment in absolute terms is six times as great? These questions are indicative of the direction in which attitudinal research may proceed to contribute to understanding of aggregate differences in national response to foreign business.

2. Attitudinal Reactions to Corporate Behavior. Research to date suggests that attitudes affecting international business-government affairs are, to a large degree, the result of influences outside the control of the individual firm—notably, various characteristics of the culture, economy, and politics of the host nation; the relation of foreign governments, especially the United States, to the host nation; and the aggregate characteristics of foreign investment in the nation. Thus, the utility of attitude studies for the firm is limited to their predictive value and contribution in understanding, which may help executives in planning corporate and individual strategies with relation to governments. However, at least to a moderate degree, it is apparent that the policies and practices which individual corporations adopt have attitudinal affects. This is a fruitful area for research to help the individual firm in its relations and because the combined effects of procedures of many corporations may be presumed to have some perceptible effect on total national reactions.

The basic approach to research for this purpose must be determination of types of attitudinal responses resulting from different patterns of corporate behavior. The work of Litvak, Maule and Robinson has provided a useful research base in identifying key variations in the latter.[16] Further research should assess attitude responses to the types of behavior differences they describe. A possible research plan would be to focus upon attitudes toward a limited number of industries, and companies within those industries, which have distinct differences in behavior patterns—particularly with respect to the critical area of effect upon control of national affairs. The main variables are the degree of foreign control for the industry and for the individual companies, and the pattern of administrative control in the operations of the firms. The attitudinal response would be determined by interviews from selected samples of elites and, perhaps, from the general public as well.

The great problem in this sort of study is the presence of complicating variables, both in corporate behavior and in influences upon the attitudes of the host nationals. This problem is likely to limit the clarity of conclusions which may be drawn from the research. However, in light of the importance of the subject, it would not appear to be an obstacle toward pursuit of research, at least as an experimental first effort. The problem, therefore, is chiefly significant in the design of the research methodology, and every effort should be made to so construct it that the complicating variables are reduced in influence.

3. Effects of Attitudes. From present knowledge we already have a fair picture of the broad effects of attitudes on international business-government affairs, in both the individual behavior of host nationals and in the appeal-support political process. This broad picture has contributed to certain equally broad guidelines for management behavior, such as avoidance of publicity which might incite public nationalistic response and thus complicate delicate negotiations.[17] The importance of such broad guidelines clearly indicates the value of greater knowledge of the influence of attitudes which will permit more refined guidance for management in direct interaction with governments and in the management of information which may affect public attitudes, which in turn influence relations with governments.

For the immediate future it would appear that further advances in this area are best made by intensive case studies. Insights into the problems and possibilities of research are provided both by two intensive case studies by Fayerweather and Kapoor[18] on specific international business-government interactions, and by other studies in related areas—notably the intensive analysis of attitudes affecting U. S. trade policy by Bauer, Poole and Dexter.[19] These studies amply demonstrate the complexity of the attitudes and the manner in which their influence is felt. It is possible that, as is the case in the Bauer study, survey work leading to hard statistical data may be useful for certain aspects of work in the immediate future. However, by and large, it would appear that the most useful gains in the near future will come from intensive case studies which provide the assurance of realism in the picture of the dynamics of attitude influences. When ten or twelve studies of substantial depth are available, we may then be in a position to generalize with hypotheses suitable for testing by survey research on broader samples.

In the meantime, the growing body of case material will in itself be highly informative for management purposes. It must be noted that development of useful case studies for this purpose requires careful research design. The Indian study by Kapoor is useful because of the degree of information about participant viewpoints obtained. This accomplishment was possible only because considerable time had passed since the event, thus reducing confidentiality barriers, and because of exceptional skill and persistance by the researcher—aided by his bicultural relationships. The Fayerweather Canadian study is less informative because the specific case remained active at the time research was being conducted, so confidential communication with participants leading to publication was not practical. These experiences indicate the importance of care in selection of situations, in order to obtain adequate information, and of care in selection of the research process.

4. Elite Attitudes in Multinational Control Institutions. A prime hypothesis of many people is that resolution of conflicts between a multinational firm and host nations may be found in some form of multinational institutional control of the firms. More specifically, it is suggested that the critical nationalistic and social-role attitudes of key elites may find satisfaction in transition to roles in multinational control institutions. This hypothesis is so important that it should be tested thoroughly. The problem lies in finding effective places for research. The transition to multinational institutions which exert really effective control is so slight that there are few situations in which any meaningful data can be collected which will contribute to any test of the hypothesis. However, there are just enough possibilities so that it may be feasible at this stage to do a little research, which, if nothing else, will test the methodologies appropriate for more intensive work as institutional development proceeds. Specific possibilities appear to lie within EEC institutions and some U. S.-Canadian arrangements–notably the automotive agreement and joint defence procurement–and, perhaps, the NATO production consortia, on other aspects of which Behrman has already done substantial work.[20] The essence of the research will lie in study of the attitudes of the host nationals immediately concerned with continuing administration and policy evolution of multinational institutions. The goal will be to determine to what degree they find satisfaction of their societal control role in the multinational aspect of this function, as distinguished from their view of it as a simple extension of their national control role, as well as the extent to which their orientation has shifted from a nation-oriented one, dominated by nationalism, toward a multinational orientation. The latter may include both broadening of the context in which national goals are achieved, and some detachment from national goals as a primary reference point and shift toward the concept of global or, at least, binational or regional optimization of societal benefits.

Chapter Three

Beyond the Multinational Corporation

Richard D. Robinson

There is a growing body of corporate history that suggests that as the market perceived by a firm becomes increasingly international, pressures operating both within and upon the firm tend to reshape its structure, decision-making process, and policies in a consistent, evolutionary way. If this be true, the impact on international relations generally could be very great. Indeed, the very survival of the nation state as a sovereign entity could perhaps be challenged one day. As was the case of the international corporation[1] before it, the multinational corporation has built into it the seeds of its own destruction. It is not in stable equilibrium either with itself or with the environment. Three points indicate this instability. First, although corporate personnel are given multinational responsibilities, characteristically they have had little international experience and no relevant technical-professional training. Second, being members of a corporate headquarters, peopled almost entirely with fellow nationals, the executives with new global responsibilities possess a set of values and a world perception that is very likely to bias their decision making. Although they may possess a willingness to allocate corporate resources optimally on a global basis, in fact, they are psychologically and legally incapable of doing so. Third, given the nonavailability of headquarters personnel equipped to operate effectively overseas, and the lower cost of employing local national managers abroad, rather than home country expatriates, plus the rapid rate of expansion often characteristic of the multinational stage, the firm employs largely local nationals to manage its new foreign facilities. It may also enter into a number of joint ventures. Hence, it lacks the capacity to maintain effective central control.

Although perhaps initially inclined for these reasons to permit greater autonomy to its associated foreign firms than did the international corporation, the multinationals—as they mature and gain international experience at the center—eventually begin to reverse the decentralization process. The benefits to be derived from integrating the worldwide movement of corporate resources becomes increasingly apparent as the contribution to corporate profits from overseas activity mounts and as the skill to effect such integration appears in corporate headquarters. It then begins to try to recapture control at the center, and to buy up partially-owned affiliates, so as to remove conflict of corporate interest inherent in local equity involvement. These trends would seem to be on a collision course.

On the one hand, we have competent and now experienced local national managers moving upward toward their respective national subsidiary ceilings in terms of promotion. On the other hand is the fact of increasingly centralized control within the multinational corporate headquarters. The local manager may respond by pushing for greater autonomy within his own operation, which is often signalled by a breakdown in communication between subsidiary and headquarters, an exaggerated importance given to environmental factors in decision making, and continued inability of the firm to maintain effective control. Or, the local manager may leave the employ of the firm. Host governments tend to support the local manager's desire for greater autonomy, for increased external control of the allocation of domestic resources sooner or later becomes politically unacceptable. The environmental factor thus, in fact, becomes unduly important.

Eventually, the multinational headquarters perceives the cost inherent in the communications breakdown, loss of control, mounting political pressures, and possible loss of key foreign managerial personnel. As it does so, nationality barriers are removed, and foreign nationals are likely to begin appearing in responsible managerial spots outside their respective national subsidiaries—first in regional headquarters if there be such, then in corporate headquarters itself.[2] (This is where the model may begin to diverge from the Japanese one, because it is almost inconceivable that non-Japanese managers could work effectively at high levels within the corporate headquarters of a Japanese corporation, particularly when one considers the system of permanent employment and relatively permanent work groups still characteristic of large Japanese corporations. How can the non-Japanese manager be thrust horizontally into such a situation and be expected to relate effectively?) Returning to our non-Japanese model, one should note that several forces combine in time to multinationalize the ownership of the multinational corporation. Among these, for the U. S.-based multinational, are: U. S. controls over direct foreign investment, a program encouraging the swap of U. S.-parent company stock for foreign assets; the foreign sale of debentures convertible to parent company stock; and the listing of parent company stock on foreign stock exchanges. For the European-based multinationals, the relatively small size of the local capital market pushes in the direction of multinational ownership, including the appeal of cross-border mergers and/or repeated joint venturing among multinationals. In addition, both in more and less developed countries, one may be compelled to recognize host society demands—often translated into political pressures—for a share in the profit derived from its market. The degree to which ownership has been, in fact, multinationalized is another inadequately researched subject for which we have no empirically-based trend line. The Harvard multinational corporate study found that, "The stock ownership of U. S.-controlled multinational enterprises is overwhelmingly in the hands of U. S. nationals. Only a very few of the outstanding shares of the parent firm—something on the order of 2 or 3 percent—are owned by foreigners."[3] But the evidence cited to support the conclusion is not convincing.

Many firms are now in this transitional state between the multinational firm and the truly transnational firm. The latter is simply a corporation which has lost its national identity, except in so far as legal restraints may have an impact upon decisions and operations. Its decisions are virtually bias-free in respect to nationality, because it is owned and managed by the nationals of more than one country. It is possibly true that, in the long run, a necessary—if not sufficient condition—for maximum corporate growth is multinational ownership and management at all levels. Thus, it is the transnational corporations which may continue to grow most rapidly.

Transnationals with annual gross sales at a multi-billion dollar level may soon not be uncommon. It has been predicted that there will be some 300 such corporations by 1985, controlling a very large part of the fixed industrial assets of the free world.[4] In fact, will they? Their sheer size—and absence of all national loyalty inherent in their multinational ownership and management—brings such corporations onto a collision course with the nation-state. Indeed, there is considerable evidence that even though governments may be promoting or permitting national mergers and industrial concentrations, increasingly they are resisting mergers and arrangements among the giant multinationals and transnationals. It is U. S.-antitrust policy to prevent mergers wherever they take place or whatever the nationality of the merging companies, if the effect of the merger would be to reduce competition significantly within the U. S. or within the foreign trade of the U. S. The European Community seems to be setting a precedent by barring the further acquisition of important national companies by large multinationals or transnationals. The Japanese have been restrictive in this regard for some time, and one sees no reason why they should shift direction. But to achieve effective political control of such giant multinational and transnational firms requires new international institutions, particularly with regard to the transnationals because of their greater growth potential and absence of any national loyalty of bias. No national government, not even an international regional agency such as the European Economic Community, can claim the right to determine the law under which a multinationally-owned and multinationally-managed corporation with resources strewn around the world can operate.

Therefore, the next stage in the evolutionary process may be the appearance of the supranational firm. Such entities must, necessarily, rest on

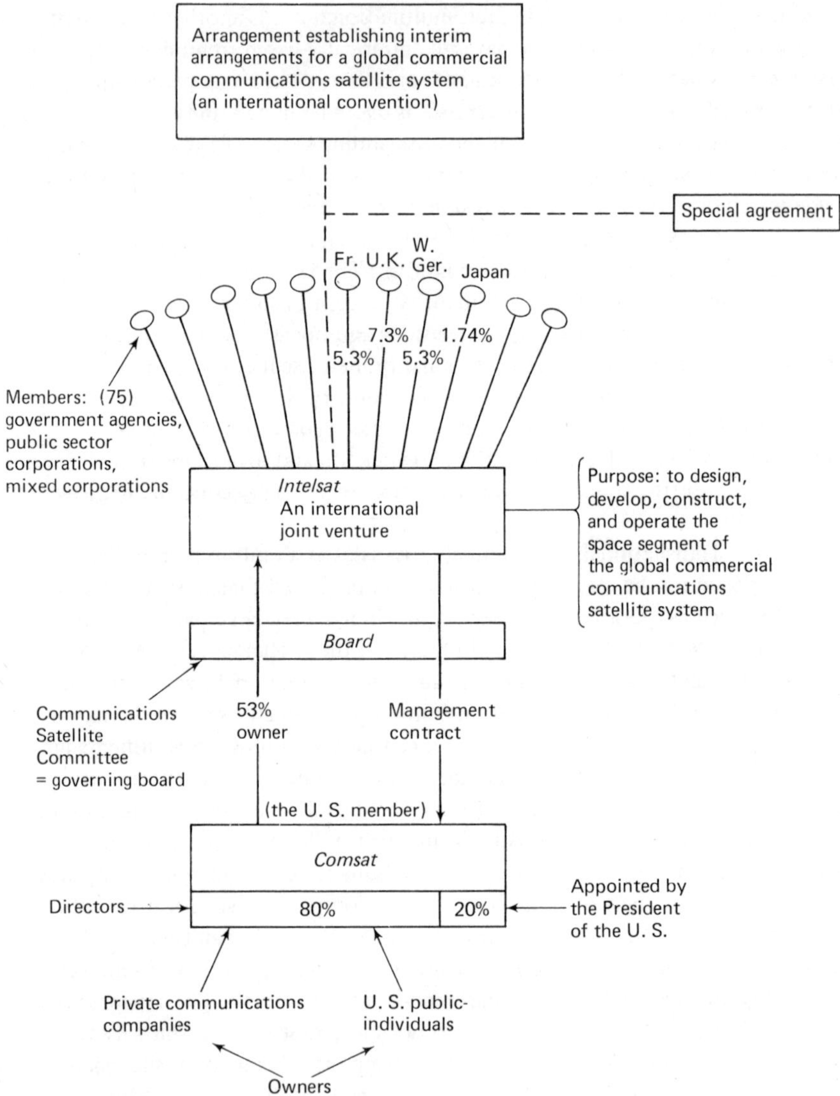

Figure 3-1. Structure of Intelsat

special intergovernmental agreements or treaties, which in each case provides the legal basis for a governing body. The only prototypes at the moment are public (the International Bank for Reconstruction and Development), and quasipublic (Intelsat, see Figure 3-1). Considered, but dropped, was the AIDCO proposal for the planning, construction, and operation of a large Middle Eastern Agro-Industrial Complex (AIDCO), which is diagrammed in Figure 3-2. One can expect two further near-term developments: (1) the emergence of a

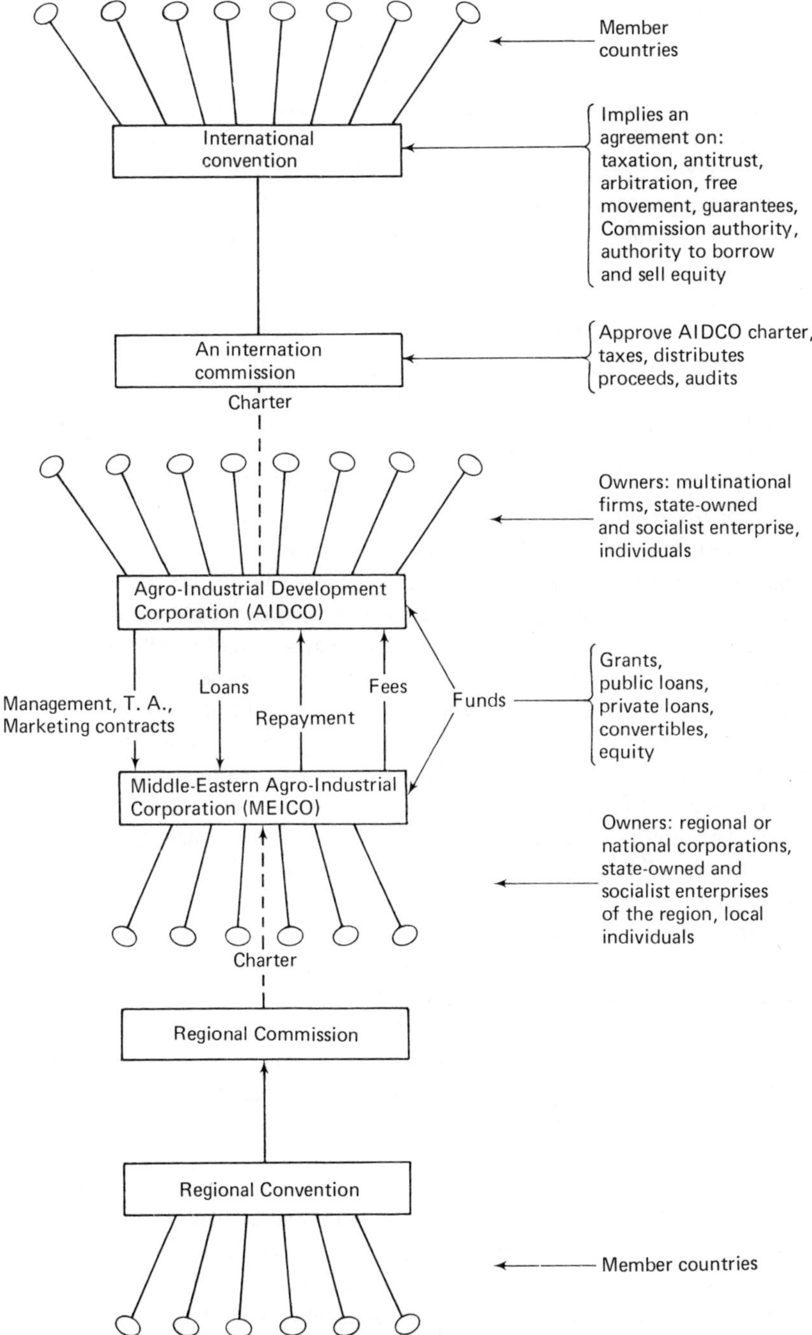

Figure 3-2. The AIDCO Project

European corporation, chartered and controlled–if not taxed–under an EEC law, and (2) the appearance of an international seabed authority, which would charter, control, and possibly tax corporations operating on the bed of the ocean. Various proposals have been made for a general international convention, under which some sort of commission would be created for chartering, controlling, and taxing of corporations satisfying certain conditions with respect to multinationality of ownership and management.

Consider the politically intolerable size of the giant transnationals within the next decade, the degree to which economic power will be concentrated in the hands of decision makers virtually unreachable by any government, the inability of single nation states–or even regional groupings–to regulate these firms. The common interest of nation-states almost compels them to participate in an effort to harmonize national policy with regard to antitrust, taxation, corporate law, and restraint-on-resource allocation. The common interest becomes irresistibly compelling if one adds the mounting pressure to internationalize political decision making, as we approach the finite limits of our global environment. Obviously, the rate of resource usage, energy consumption, atmospheric and oceanic pollution can only be resolved on a global basis. Finally, there is no evidence leading one to believe that the giant transnational corporation will voluntarily incorporate any mechanism rendering it socially responsible, other than through the marketplace, which, even within the U. S., is perceived as inadequate in respect to antitrust, consumer safety, education, health, and environment. It would appear that either the nation-states, in concert, dominate the giant transnational, or the reverse will occur. Bear in mind that the former implies an international convention, creating a body of basic law and a representative body with adequate resources to control these corporations. The international corporate law may specify, for example, that national shareholders will be represented on the corporate board by a government appointee approved by those shareholders. Given such a system of international law and control, the possibility of a truly supranational corporation appears.

If nations find it impossible to collaborate to this degree, they are likely to act to restrain further transnational corporate growth; first, by forbidding further mergers and acquisitions, and–if this is seen as an inadequate impediment to further growth–then by expropriating local assets. Most vulnerable, of course, would be integrated plants in mature industries serving, primarily, the local market and belonging to transnational corporations in which there would be little or no local equity involvement.

Or, it may just be that the pattern apparently emerging in Japan, for some of the reasons already suggested, will prove so profitable that the large North American and Western European-based multinationals and transnationals will be induced to change their structure. What seems to be developing in Japan is the multinational *association* (see Figure 3-3). At the center is a Japanese-owned and managed corporation, which is linked internationally

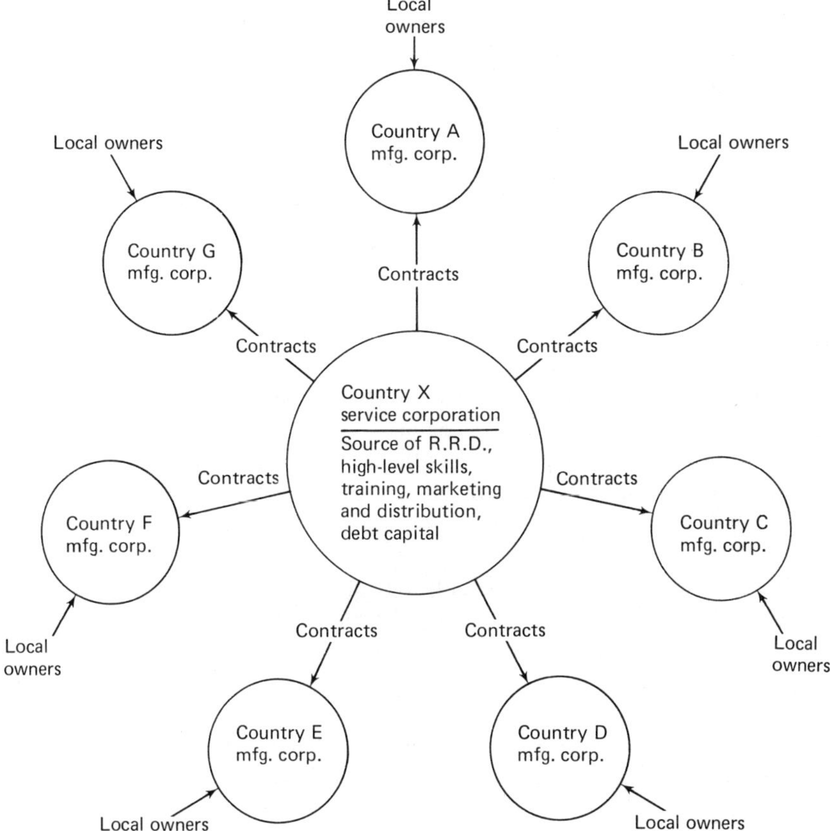

Figure 3-3. The Multinational or Transnational Association (Japanese)

Note: If the Country X Service Corporation is owned and managed essentially by country X nationals, it is *a multinational* association; if owned largely by the associated firms and managed, at least in part, by them, it is a *transnational* association.

by a web of contractual relations with largely locally-owned and managed associated firms. The center supplies capital-intensive, scarce resources—such as new technology (i. e., research and development, plus the training of local nationals), management and managerial training, international marketing services, purchase and sale contracts, debt capital, and, possibly, initial high-risk (entrepreneurial) equity, which is later withdrawn. Such an association could become transnational if the central corporation were owned by the associated foreign firms. The increase in public-sector or profit-sharing enterprise in both less and more developed countries, whether ideologically socialist or otherwise, also suggests that this pattern may indeed be the wave of future, that the multinational and transnational corporation as presently conceived will prove to be a relatively short-lived transitional form. Both legal restraints and higher profit levels to be realized by those firms, concentrating on providing scarcer, more capital-intensive inputs via contract, suggest this conclusion. The higher profits appear because the firm based in an industrially-developed country can concentrate its resources on producing those services in shortest supply, which, therefore, should command the highest prices. In economic terms, it is maximizing its monopoly rent on these relatively scarce factors of production. One might suggest that it is also minimizing its political risk for, from the point of view of the recipient country, benefits and costs would be specifically linked and not generalized in a stream of dividends. The contract route also permits a systematic periodic renegotiation as the benefit-cost ratios shift, which, for instance, would be signalled when another firm is prepared to provide comparable inputs at less cost. It is for this reason that one might anticipate the demise of many of the giant multinational and transnational firms.

Another pressure pushing in the direction of the association firm is the multitude of regulations appearing in the less developed countries encouraging–or requiring–the spin-off of all, or most, foreign ownership after a specified number of years. The list of such countries includes India, Indonesia, the Philippines, and the Andean Pact countries (Colombia, Chile, Peru, Bolivia, and Ecuador). Because Japan is investing more heavily, *relatively,* in the less developed countries than the U. S. or Europe, Japanese firms are likely to feel this pressure more directly, thereby pushing the Japanese in the direction of the multinational association.

Thus, one is driven to the conclusion that either a mechanism must be created to provide international political control over the giant transnational firms which could constitute an important next step in the long road to effective world government, or the Japanese model of multinational associations will dominate. As these associations become transnational in nature–at which point the Japanese may find themselves at a disadvantage–the need for some form of international political control will again arise. Such control is also dictated by the environmental problem and the global-resource allocation process it implies. So, following either route, one day the pressure of world business is likely to force the nation-states into a posture of cooperation thus far unknown.

Implications of Research

It would appear important to determine whether the pressures suggested in the preceding pages are, in fact, building up within the international business systems to levels that are forcing the suggested structural and political changes. The hypotheses follow:

Hypotheses:

1) The administrative structure of the firm varies consistently as foreign sales increase in relation to domestic sales. This evolution is a function of

pressures generated within the firm and of pressures exerted by the economic-political environment;

2) This variation follows an evolutionary pattern, the stages of which may be designated as domestic, foreign-oriented, international, transitional multinational, multinational, and transnational. Alternative forms following the multinational may be the multinational and transnational association;
3) The degree to which control over foreign operations is centralized in corporate headquarters is consistently related to the evolutionary stage with which the firm is most closely identified.

Significance of Research: If the hypotheses are supported by the research, we will have established an evolutionary model of organizational behavior of predictive value, if the effective market for goods and services becomes increasingly international, as seems likely. The fact that international production (that is, the total value of production of industrial plants owned by nationals foreign to the country in which the plants are located) is estimated to be between one-quarter and one-third of gross world production, underscores the importance of anticipating the most likely structure and control centers of the owning corporations. Many public policy implications follow, including those policies most likely to maximize the international transfer of technology.

Methodology. In the year 1956-8, the author studied 131 U. S.-based corporations in detail. This study was based on personal interviews with key officials, and analysis of written records. Although the sample was obviously not selected on a purely random basis, it was sufficiently large and diverse (in terms of industry, size and structure of firm, importance of foreign markets, length, and depth of experience in foreign operations) as to provide a good cross section. It would indeed be extremely unlikely that this sample is unique in any significant dimension.

Because Japanese industry may represent an important variant in the evolutionary pattern that is hypothesized, it will be necessary to include a Japanese study. For this purpose, it is proposed to conduct personal interviews in every tenth firm listed in "Japan's 500 leading industrial corporations" (published annually by *President Magazine,* Tokyo).

In that the purpose of the study is to relate the internationalization of the relevant market with changes in corporate structure and control, it would be misleading to base the study on a statistical analysis because one is dealing with sets of pressures and responses—that is, processes—that cannot be quantified realistically.

It is proposed to use the 1956-58 data as a baseline for a restudy of these same corporations in order to ascertain

1) Changes in administrative structure;
2) The degree to which the relevant market has become international;

3) Changes in the locale of essential elements of control in respect to foreign operations. These may be defined as:
   a) What to produce, where, with what inputs, for sale where, and under what conditions?
   b) What R&D to undertake, where, and on what scale?
   c) The recruitment, development, and assignment of individuals possessing high-level skills, including managerial—and, hence, their remuneration.
   d) The negotiation of working conditions with labor (now that international labor organizations are appearing).
   e) The incurring of large-scale financial commitment.
   f) Intra-subsidiary movements of goods, services, and people.
   g) The reporting of profits and losses.
4) Changes in the nationality of corporate ownership;
5) Changes in nationality of managers exercising essential control;
6) Changes in the nationality of directors;
7) Perceived major environmental pressures;
8) Perceived pressures within the corporation;
9) Changes in personnel policy in respect to overseas operations (selection, preparation, promotion, mobility, remuneration);
10) Changes in ownership policy;
11) Level of sophistication of environmental analysis;
12) Degree of political flexibility vis-a-vis overseas activities;
13) Objective measures of centralization (number of organizational levels between the chief executive and the heads of foreign units, implementation of profit centers, existence of formal task descriptions with authority specifications, perceived degree of autonomy given to foreign units by headquarters' managers, degree of standardized information transmission);
14) Risk perceptions (rate of return thresholds, payback periods required, shifting of risk via investment guarantee);
15) Management response to forced spin-off of ownership (Cartegena Decision, Indonesia, Philippines, etc.);
16) Management's anticipation of future corporate growth.

Chapter Four

Can the Multinational Enterprise Gain Acceptability through Industrial Integration

Jack N. Behrman

A basic question posed by any institution which holds power concerns its legitimacy—i. e., its right to exercise that power. The multinational enterprise (MNE) has power through its many options in the location of industrial operations, its movement of funds, determination of technology, and trade patterns. But such an enterprise has no visible legitimacy as it is now structured, and as it wishes to operate. The legal basis for the multinational enterprise is built up out of national law and international agreements concerning the right of establishment, which include guarantees of "comity" or "national treatment." No intergovernmental agreement is the basis for, or protects the rights of, the multinational enterprise. The entity, therefore, has no "international" legitimacy and can claim only the rights granted by national governments to its separate affiliates.

Even without a legal or political legitimacy, the enterprise can gain a certain legitimacy by operating in a manner acceptable to those it affects. The argument of this paper relates to whether the multinational enterprise might gain acceptability through meeting the problems of industrial integration. We start with several propositions, which are not argued and which probably do not require further research. From that point, an assessment is made of why there is much confusion in the realm of industrial integration; these "whys" arise from a lack of theoretical guidance and do need much more research. We follow with a characterization of the policies toward industrial integration, which also need additional investigation. The potential role of the MNE in industrial integration is then hypothesized. Finally, a set of recommendations is offered, which need substantial further argumentation and research before they can be implemented.

Propositions:

1) The multinational enterprise is characterized by a policy of integrating affiliates among themselves, with the parent to achieve the least-cost

operation, to serve the market (national, regional, or international) in the most efficient manner. It is, therefore, an especially apt mechanism for accelerating industrial integration.

2) Industrial integration is necessary and desirable to achieve satisfactory economic growth—i.e., at an appropriate rate, with appropriate composition, and without overcapacity. Industrial integration is needed to achieve economies of scale in production within national economies or among members of a regional group, and, even more necessary, to gain levels of efficiency permitting exports to the world market.
3) Industrial integration will accelerate the growth of multinational enterprises, for they will find the economic atmosphere most suitable to their policies of integrating affiliates. Conversely, the growth of multinational enterprises will accelerate industrial integration, but under the guidance of the MNES.
4) The more rapid growth of multinational enterprises under policies of industrial integration will make even more visible in host countries the fact that *control* resides outside and that the benefits are determined and distributed by (if not to) foreigners. This visibility will lead to increasing dissatisfaction with the role of the multinational enterprise in host countries; this, in turn, will lead to imposition of restrictions and the construction of competing multinational enterprises. (The evidence for this proposition can be found not only in the developing countries, but also most recently in Europe, not to mention Canada.)
5) Industrial integration at the hands of the multinational enterprise will tend to benefit the richer, more advanced countries, compared to the lesser developed countries. (This is evident not only among the presently "industrialized" and "nonindustrialized" countries of the Northern vs. Southern Hemisphere, but also within the developing regions. For example, Latin American integration has been slowed by the fact that it was soon evident that Argentina, Brazil, and Mexico were gaining the greater portion of the industrial benefits. One study of the more than 500 industrial companies in Latin America, which were exporting over $100,000 annually during the late 1960s showed that these companies were concentrated in three countries—155 in Argentina, 144 in Brazil, and 114 in Mexico; of the total, just under half were foreign-owned, with American affiliates outnumbering other foreign affiliates by 2 to 1.[1] As a consequence of this concentration of industrial activity, national governments will insist on adopting "industrial policies" aimed at redistribution of industrial activity that provides for some acceptable degree of "reciprocity" or "sharing."
6) In order for governments to use the multinational enterprise in pursuit of appropriate forms of industrial integration, the MNE must first become acceptable as an institution. To accomplish this, it must be shown to be serving the needs and desires of the countries in which it is located.

Otherwise, it will be restricted, rejected, or dismembered; in this event, it could no longer operate as effectively in an integrating fashion.

The following parts of the argument consist of hypotheses that require further research, in order to point the way in which the MNE may become acceptable.

Lack of Guidelines

The hypothesis of this section is that governments find it difficult to redirect the activities of the MNE toward industrial integration, because they do not have any clear or acceptable guidelines. Theoretical justifications which have been used to support the location of industry by free-market principles are no longer acceptable to the governments involved (if they ever were).

To test this hypothesis will require a more searching investigation of the relevance and acceptability of the theories of trade, integration, welfare, and economic development than has been given them. Each of these has been gestated within Western economic thought and more avidly supported by American economists than European or Latin American. But only the U. S. government has grounded its policies within these theories, and even it seems to find them less relevant than before, when special problems arise, such as handling textile import pressures.

Historically, the "law of comparative advantage" has been the rationale for decisions as to location of industrial activity regionally and internationally. A region or nation that could produce an item relatively most cheaply should produce it for sale to the world. The criterion underlying this law is that of efficiency: the most efficient production was to be sought as a means of maximizing total output. But the assumptions necessary to make the law of comparative advantage operative are many, and have seldom been in existence. Apart from assumptions concerning the maintenance of peace (i. e., an abstraction from the national security argument), the most important are that (a) reasonably free competition exists, (b) free markets obtain, (c) all relevant costs are included in the price, (d) countries are more or less in the same stages of development, and (e) economic growth is either *the* goal or *the* primary means to all other goals of the country. Given these assumptions, growth can be obtained best by seeking the most efficient means and location of production.

Under these assumptions, the law of comparative advantage leads to a policy of free trade among nations, and among regions within a nation. Consequently, industry is located where it can achieve "least costs" of production and distribution to the markets. If the assumed conditions do not exist, policies are supposed to be directed toward achieving these desired conditions so that free trade can be instituted, and industry located according to comparative advantage; the highest efficiency then can be obtained.

It is increasingly recognized that not all relevant costs will be imposed on the market mechanism, though this is theoretically possible. To do so would require not only that all environmental costs be included, but also that costs of the movement of manpower and its retraining be imposed on the company—as well as costs of pensions, health care for workers, and, most importantly, the costs of urban agglomeration and concentration that arise from concentration of industry in the "most efficient" locations. Since these costs are not borne directly by industry, it cannot be said that they achieve the "least-cost" solutions for the economy; they are achieved only for the company, given the existing situation.

The fact that countries exist in widely different stages of development means that they are seeking to alter the "free trade" location of industry, so as to achieve a "more equal" status. This is the goal of all development policies among the lesser advanced countries. Development policies are aimed at changing comparative advantages; this is a dynamic process which never ends. It is impossible, therefore, to determine at any given time what the comparative advantages will be or what the most efficient location of industry will be.

This is probably just as well, for the criteria which societies and governments impose on industrial location are wider than that of efficiency. The "first-best" solution of the economists is simply not adequate; it is neither "first" nor "best" in the view of government officials, nor to the people to whom they are responsible. Of equal, or sometimes greater, weight are the goals of autonomy, of participation, and of equity. These cannot be sought through a free market; they require considered policies concerning industrial development and integration.

The theory of economic integration is also of no help in pursuit of these three objectives, for it also is based on the law of comparative advantage and how not to do much violence to it internationally, while limiting free trade to a given region. Economic welfare theory is virtually bankrupt, in terms of policy; it assumes that efficiency criteria are the "first-best" and that with a larger pie all can be better off. Under this prescription, industry can be located where it is most "efficient" under market conditions, and then the benefits can be distributed so that all in the region are better off. But it provides no means for assuring that the benefits of greater production are distributed, so that all are, in fact, better off than before. The distribution is never carried out effectively; but even if it were, the criterion of participation would not be met, nor would that of autonomy.

Basically, economic theories of trade and welfare (and even integration) assume an orientation toward a "one-world" situation that is itself a "value" (desired goal) within the economist's supposedly "value-free" discipline. To reject the efficiency criterion as "first-best" is to relegate economic arguments concerning location of industrial activity to a secondary or tertiary position, leaving the economist with little to contribute and governments with a need to search elsewhere for guidelines.

Location theory itself is not much help. This theory has emphasized a variety of commercial, institutional, and resource considerations that were not readily subsumed under economic theory, but which also do not get to the issues raised here.

The lack of satisfactory guidelines is evident in the unwillingness of the Central American Common Market to follow prescriptions of traditional theory in the location of industry; of the Latin American Free Trade Area (LAFTA), to continue across-the-board duty reductions, which concentrated the benefits in the more advanced countries; and of the European Economic Community to set up a European Investment Bank and a Social Fund to redress the imbalance of industrial activity and the social costs of economic integration; in the policies of the European Coal and Steel Community (ECSC), to regularize production and rationalize steel production and coal mining; and in the U. S.-Canadian auto agreement. As under the ECSC, the U. S.-Canadian agreement, and now the complementation agreements under LAFTA, what is sought is a means of determining the location of industry that does not follow "free trade" prescriptions. Whether or not the result is more or less "efficient" is difficult to say, since the conditions are changed by the investment and location decisions; it is conceivable that the other objectives have been, or can be, obtained with little or no cost in efficiency. It would be most useful to study the trade-offs between the "efficiency" criterion and the other objectives of governments.

The hypothesis that there is potentially little loss of efficiency in programmed location of industry is derived from the increasing capability of many economies to support a wide variety of industrial activities. It is perfectly feasible to locate production of many product lines or services in one of many countries, for both local and world consumption—e. g., shoes, textiles, electronics, some chemicals, pharmaceuticals, office machines, toys, paper products, banking, airlines, and so on. In fact, the more that similar stages of economic development are achieved, the less likely it is that any one region will have a comparative advantage in specific product lines. Specialization will be necessary simply because of the different sizes of national economies. But, what nations specialize in is likely to be a result of historical development rather than economic necessity.

Governments are now concerned to reduce the historical pressures, to change the development pattern and, thus, obtain the goals of autonomy, participation, and equity, while maintaining efficiency. They are doing this by means of a series of interventionist policies affecting the location of industrial activity. These policies lack a theoretical base and are not harmonized among nations, leaving them competing for the new industrial activities over the world.

Location Incentives

Given the variety of incentives offered to domestic and foreign investors, a second major hypothesis is that harmonization of these incentives will be necessary before industrial integration policies could be formed regionally or internationally. A corollary would be that harmonization is required as part of a common policy toward the MNE.

Governments have, for many decades (even centuries), interfered with location decisions of companies for the purpose of achieving objectives other than market efficiency. Mercantilist policies were directed toward achieving industrialization within a given developmental goal, including assurance of staple supplies to urban communities and export capacity in order to obtain gold. The "national economics" of Friedrich List was much more acceptable to European countries, even during the period of the Pax Britannica, than the "free trade" policies of England. Since World War II, moves toward "freer trade" were accepted only because of strong pressure of the U. S., which was willing for the two postwar decades to underwrite economic growth and stability in the reconstructing and developing countries. But, the idea of free trade and market determination of the location of industrial activity has not been widely accepted anywhere in the world outside of the U. S., and, possibly, Canada. Germany has been closest to accord with U. S. ideas, of the European countries in the postwar period, but it has not relinquished interventionist policies toward industrial location.

Efforts to achieve industrial development require attention to the integration of industrial activity at three levels: national, regional, and international. At national levels, industrial development has proceeded far enough in some countries so that what is now sought are largely modifications in industrial growth patterns; for others, programs are required to develop an industrial base. Regionally, some countries are now integrating in ways that will require coordination of industrial development. Moves at the third level, that of international industrial integration, are wholly lacking.

At the national level, we find a variety of incentives in the form of subsidies, tax rebates or waivers, gifts of plant sites, etc., which are designed to attract new industry and to induce it to locate in selected areas. The multinational enterprises, coming onto the scene relatively recently, are in a better position to respond to such inducements than are purely "domestic" companies. Not only do they bring "new" industry, in the sense of something additional, but they also are willing to consider locations not so attractive to national industry. The MNEs, therefore, are often more responsive to national industrial incentives than are domestic companies; consequently, they are seldom the subject of complaints at the *local* level; local communities feel themselves fortunate to have any new industries.

At the level of regional industrial integration, the multinational enterprises are already credited with a substantial contribution to European integration, responding more readily to the reduction of barriers than did European companies. Not only have they responded earlier to the idea of Europe as a single market, but also they have taken into Europe the American policy of plant decentralization, which permits locating operations at several national sites or among European countries, thereby spreading the benefits of industrialization. A similar result would occur in Latin America if the governments really moved toward regional integration. As it is, their national orientations prevent a substantial move on the part of the multinationals to expand intraregional trade and investment, locking operations of their affiliates together.

At the international level, there are no direct efforts toward industrial integration. Provisions of the GATT and the OECD leave industrial location to the decisions of companies. There are no "codes of investment" as proposed under the International Trade Organization (ITO) of 1949 or more recently, and there are no agreed measures for attraction of international investment. The only industrial agreements have arisen from ad hoc "trouble" situations, such as those surrounding the textile industry. Consequently, we are meeting the problems of international location of industry and over- or under-capacity rather ineffectively. Within this setting, the multinational enterprise is claimed to have the potential for being the primary means of achieving international industrial integration under the criterion of efficiency—that is, it can achieve the greatest efficiency for the world economy if it were allowed to follow least-cost principles. It would be highly useful to determine whether, in fact, the MNE is such an efficient mechanism and what its measures of efficiency are.

Acceptability of the MNE

Given the above propositions and setting, the third hypothesis is that, even if the MNE were the most efficient means, pursuit of the other criteria of equity, autonomy, and participation require either some governmental activity or guidelines for the behavior of the MNE to make it an acceptable vehicle. Acceptability (and legitimacy) is gained by the MNE doing what is considered appropriate by the relevant groups affected in pursuit of its desired goals. Although, there are three separate arenas for industrial integration—national, regional, and international[2]—the relevant groups are still within the nation-state. They will decide what is good at both the regional and international levels. The MNE, therefore, must find a way to accommodate to the desires of citizens of nation-states as to the location of industry within the nations, and among those nations integrating regionally and internationally. The criteria of acceptability will not necessarily be the same at each level.

For those who see the future of the world in "internationalism" or "federalism," the MNE is a highly acceptable institution because it is seen as divorceable from national interests and constraints. The criterion for economic activity, which is employed by the internationalists, is solely that of "efficiency," for they have accepted the concepts of welfare theory that states a larger pie benefits all. They do not doubt that the MNEs *can* increase efficiency and productivity over the world. But, "efficiency" is not a concept that can be divorced from the larger concepts of what is produced and for whom. Though internationalists finesse the issue of "benefit sharing," they cannot do so without accepting whatever equity the market dictates (or the MNE through its decisions), giving over to the judgment of MNE managements what to produce and how. A consequence could be that products were made and sold that did not meet the needs or desires of the people, thereby "wasting" resources—meaning, inefficient use of national resources. The claim that the MNE is "efficient" is a claim housed within concepts of income distribution, economic and political power, resource availability, and product demand, in which the companies themselves determine who does, and who gets, what, To claim that the MNE achieves maximum "efficiency" in a system that is considered both inequitable and "inefficient" in meeting society's needs is not to claim much, and certainly not to achieve acceptability for the MNE.

At the regional level, to consider that the MNE will produce an acceptable integration of industry among member countries, without governmental guidance, is again to presuppose that MNE judgments are acceptable to the members. They are not, necessarily. The MNE must be guided—as should all other enterprise—to accord with the policy prescriptions of the member countries. It is, as stated above, more likely to be able to respond readily than local companies, but it is not always inclined to do so. The evidence obtained from LAFTA is that just half of the largest 500 companies in intra-regional industrial trade are affiliates of international companies; Latin American-owned companies kept pace in large measure with their international counterparts. Among the international companies involved in intraregional exports, the U. S. affiliates outnumbered the Europeans 2 to 1, but out-exported them only by 3 to 2. The U. S.-owned companies accounted for about one-fourth of intraregional industrial exports, but comprised one-third the total number of companies.[3]

At the national level, the MNEs are also capable of accelerating industrial integration, fostering consumer industries, assisting supplier firms, developing materials supplies, providing business for transport, and other infrastructure necessary for industrial development. But they do not always do so. Contrarily, some MNE-affiliates are established to import materials and supplies from the parent, or to export materials to the parent with little processing. Rather than helping to integrate the host economy at the national level, they are integrating that economy with the world economy or that of the home country. It is difficult for the MNE to gain acceptability in this fashion.

The MNE faces a difficult task, therefore, in gaining acceptability at all levels of industrial integration, especially since its own corporate interest militates in favor of international integration, based on "efficiency" criteria. To take other criteria into account is to do so at the cost of corporate interest and may even reduce profits. But, not to take them into account will reduce acceptability and risk the use of constraining interventions by governments which are likely to overreact.

To achieve acceptability, the MNE must take into full consideration what it is that national groups want. From the standpoint of operations, what is wanted is an appropriate mixture of equity, efficiency, participation, and control. Each of these is sought at all three levels of industrial integration. And each can be obtained through different operations or aspects of the MNE. For example, control can be exercised either through ownership or participation in management—through private channels or government—and on a daily basis or through setting of guidelines and policies to follow. Participation can be obtained at the ownership or management levels, in R&D activities, and in labor committees. Equity can be achieved through profit-sharing, through pricing, trade, assistance to secondary and supplier industries, finance, technology, and tax policies. Efficiency will undoubtedly be sought, but will be left largely to management to achieve *within* the other constraints.

It would be useful to determine the trade-offs among these four objectives. It may be hypothesized that control is the most important, for with it all else can be obtained. But since few countries argue that they must obtain majority control of all foreign-owned affiliates, what is sought is merely sufficient control to alter decisions that affect the nature of participation, the kinds of technologies used, the distribution of benefits, and the trade-offs (if any) against efficiency. The more control demanded at the national level, the less feasible it is for the MNE to achieve the levels of efficiency necessary for any affiliate to compete successfully internationally. Thus, there is a limit to the reduction of efficiency feasible if world-market competition is important, as it is for most countries.

Though control is probably the most important, it does not require ownership; it can be exercised by controls and in specific areas rather than as part of managements' overall responsibilities. What the MNEs should seek, therefore, is a mixture of national control and managerial responsibility that produces acceptability. It is hypothesized that attention to the problems of industrial integration could gain an acceptable role for the MNE.

To this point, we have hypothesized that the MNE can gain legitimacy (acceptability), through provision of appropriate levels of equity participation, and efficiency, and that these objectives are more readily achieved through harmonized or concerted policies concerned with industrial integration.

Methodological Approach

Given the different levels of argument proposed here, different methodologies will be required. To assess the relevance of past theoretical guidelines, a careful examination of the assumptions and value-propositions underlying trade and integration theories would be required, laying bare their irrelevance for present problems which combine the developing world with the advanced countries. This theoretical analysis would be accompanied by a further assessment of the absence of any adequate "welfare" theory to guide the distribution of benefits among countries. While some empirical work exists, the major thrust of this part of the research would be to demonstrate, as conclusively as possible, the poverty of economic theory which is asserted to be "valueless" when the policies necessary to implement those theories embody extensive, specific, and significant "value systems."

A second approach would be strictly empirical—a careful examination and comparison of the national (and regional) industrial policies of the major countries which are host to the MNE, which would be used to show how they have affected the location of industry, the patterns of trade and flow of finance. From this research would come the capacity to make a priori judgments as to the distribution of benefits of industrial development among and within both developing and advanced countries.

The third segment would involve careful analysis of the decision-making processes within the MNE as to industrial location, patterns of trade, and funds flows. Much of this research has already been done, but not necessarily with the purpose of answering the kinds of questions posed here. The questions raised would be directed toward determining what would be necessary to alter the decisions so as to assure equitable distribution of the benefits benefits of industrial development—"equitable" defined in terms of some criteria of sharing of employment, trade, technology, etc. From these studies—conducted in terms of actual moves made by MNEs, as well as in terms of "hypothetical" situations posed to company officials—should come guidelines which could achieve high levels of efficiency and equity among countries, and of industrial integration. To determine such guidelines, however, would require interviews with both company and government officials.

Recommendations

If the hypotheses set forth here prove correct, it would seem that the following actions would gain acceptability for the MNE:

1) National governments should develop industrial policies which provide clear guidance to foreign (and local) investors concerning the industrial sectors which are to be developed and promoted, and the incentives that are to be extended to private companies. This delineation of industrial policies should be extended to regional bodies as well; and, internationally, at least on a selected sectoral basis—e. g., covering textiles, shoes, electronics, etc.
2) For developing countries, particularly, the role of the private sector in industrial development should be clearly defined. In many countries there is still considerable indecision as to what roles the private sector will be permitted to play; this leads to repeated changing of the basic rules of the game, which will, in the long run, frustrate the activities of all companies, including foreign investors.

3) In determining industrial policies, governments should be careful to make explicit the criteria by which location of industry will be fostered or guided. The criteria would probably include its employment-generating capacity, its use of skilled or semiskilled labor, the kinds of technology employed, its export-generating capacity—in line with major concerns of governments. In addition, criteria concerning entrance of foreign investors will probably include means of determining the appropriate division of earnings among owners in different countries and of revenue among governments.
4) The MNE should seek to solve the excruciating problems of high unemployment in certain countries of the world, to spread technological advances (including the capacity to generate new techniques), and to distribute the benefits of industrial advance among those served by the MNE.
5) New organizational structure within and among governments should be created to promote industrial integration and use the capacities of the MNE. National plans should pay closer attention to sectoral industrial development. Regional commissions should be established to oversee industrial integration in key sectors (as in the European Community and the Andean Group). And a new organization should be created internationally to provide information, to develop concerted policies, and to promulgate guidelines on the role of the MNE in key industrial sectors.[4]
6) The MNE must first recognize the problems posed here, then take the initiative and discuss them with governments. Not to do so will mean that governmental actions will be harsher than necessary, more uncertain, and likely to frequent changes in policy. The more pressing problems of employment, technology, selection of appropriate product lines, trade patterns, and revenue should be raised immediately, but placed against a longer-term dialogue concerning equity, participation, and control.
7) As a means of showing that they have the interests of host countries at heart, and of showing that they can take useful initiatives in solving very difficult problems of economic growth, the MNEs should identify projects for which their talents are especially useful—depollution, river-basin development, resource development in the ocean bed, aerospace exploration, satellite communication, innovation of complex systems to solve urban growth problems, etc. Such initiatives would demonstrate that their interests are "problem solving" rather than mere profitability, and governments would respond with arrangements that permitted acceptable levels of profit. These arrangements have precedents in various infrastructure projects within Latin America and in the NATO and European coproduction projects. Some further study is required to determine how such projects might be extended beyond governmental procurement and financing. But acceptance of the MNE is worth the effort.

What has been sought in this discussion are means of demonstrating that the MNE is, in fact, working for the interests of the people it affects, so that it becomes acceptable and its power legitimized. The recommendations would involve a reduction of MNE power, as compared to the hopes of some internationalists who conceive of the MNE as a sort of private international government, supplanting nation-states. But internationalism, if it comes, will be built on the foundation of strong nation-states—not on weak ones or the absence of them. There is no effective way to organize the world, other than through pyramiding governmental entities that represent progressively larger segments of the total population. Nations were not built by destroying local governments or state governments. And nation-states will not wither away in favor of some supranational entity, much less in favor of multinational enterprises.

Therefore, the MNE must find an accommodation with governments—at present, on the national level. It can do so by demonstrating a capacity to help meet industrial development problems locally, nationally, regionally, and internationally. To stress only its capacity to achieve international integration is to move in a direction national governments will not accept, unless it can be shown that national interests, in terms of participation and equity, are also served. The MNE can take the initiative in demonstrating its ability to take these interests into account, or it will come under increasing surveillance and control. Even if it is to be so constrained, early initiatives by the MNE will demonstrate that it does not have to be dragged forcibly into the newer world of corporate responsibility, but can, on its own, assume a responsibility for the problems of industrial development and social imporvement in such a way as to gain continued acceptability.

Chapter Five

The Engagement of Host Government Interests upon the Entry of Foreign Business

Richard D. Robinson

The need for a new set of skills on the part of the international manager emerges from the desire manifest by many governments to regulate the entry of alien business interests. Rightly or wrongly, these governments represent the view that some projected involvements by alien business are more desirable than others. Therefore, the manager attempting to gain entry for his firm (or to qualify it for such incentives as tax holidays, guaranteed repatriation rights, or duty-free imports), must justify what his firm proposes to do. He must do so not merely on the basis of technical feasibility and internal financial profit projections satisfactory to owners, directors, and top management, but also in terms of the criteria established by the relevant political authorities. As time passes, these criteria would appear to be less and less of subjective nature to be satisfied by personal favor. Rather, with increasing frequency, the criteria are specified in objective terms, purporting to satisfy some priority of national values. These may require the foreign manager to think and speak in terms of such unfamiliar phrases—that is, possibly unfamiliar to him—as balance of payment effect, national income effect, externalities and linkages, employment effect, the stimulation of local entrepreneurial capacity, the scheduled transfer of skills, the phased transfer of management and ownership. These latter terms imply emphasis upon—and hence skills related to—the selection and training of local nationals, the shifting of authority, the identification of local entrepreneurs, the development of a local capital market.

The schedule, on which basis these various criteria will be satisfied, is frequently the subject of negotiation with government upon initial entry, either as a condition for entry and/or the enjoyment of various benefits—or, the reverse, the avoidance of penalties. Among the penalties may be the loss of ownership and of control associated with ownership, although continued control via contract or a dispersed majority ownership may remain feasible.

Foreign business entry—including direct investment—in many countries is taking on the appearance of a negotiated contract. To negotiate relatively liberal conditions, the international manager must be sufficiently sophisticated to be able to demonstrate convincingly that a lower cost/benefit ratio could not be achieved by changing some relevant parameter, such as ownership structure, control relationships, source of capital and other resources, rate of skill and technology transfer, anticipated profit and/or fee levels, marketing and pricing strategy, the technology to be utilized and the scale of production, degree of vertical and horizontal integration. Nor is this a one-shot type of calculation, for overtime capabilities, the externalities, and flows of resources are very likely to shift significantly. This dynamic quality should be taken into account. Of interest is the frequency with which company negotiators may find highly sophisticated analysts on the government side of the table—individuals with advanced degrees from prestigious foreign universities and with widening experience. For the company, the "old hand" is no longer an effective protagonist.

Some of the national programs of interest are discussed separately below.

Thailand

Since 1960, the government of Thailand has been using a merit ratio system for selecting industrial projects—foreign and domestic—which warrant this promotional status and, hence, various benefits. The basis on which this merit ratio is calculated is given in Table 5-1.

It was reported in 1970 that the Thai Board of Investment had rarely granted promotion status to any project with a merit ratio of less than 5:1. The ratio for all projects granted promotion status was estimated between 7:1 to 8:1. It should be noted that the ratio has an important built-in bias; it favors any project with large local participation. The result is that only about 4 percent of the projects approved up to 1970 had been wholly foreign-owned. The merit ratio system obviously gives no plus points for externalities, to strategically-selected industries with respect to their linkage effects. Additionally, the net saving of foreign exchange overtime is not considered, in that the long-term servicing of capital is not included. Despite their merit rating, the Thai Board of Investment has pursued the policy of withholding promotional status from saturated industries. As of 1970, this situation had developed in 12 industries. All in all, the Thai investment promotion program has been fairly successful, some $850 million having been invested over a 10-year period, of which 30 percent was foreign.[1]

Indonesia

According to the 1967 foreign investment law dealing with the investment of foreign capital, alien ownership in Indonesian enterprises must be extinguished within thirty years of entry, or sooner, if so specified in the entry agreement. In addition, when the capital is entirely foreign, enterprises

Table 5-1. Analytical Method to Assess Merits of Industrial Project (Thailand)

			Estimated on an Annual Basis
(1)	*Total value of output* (price x quantity)[a]		....
(2)	*Deduct:* Imported raw materials	....	
(3)	Salaries to foreign personnel	....	
(4)	Depreciation on imported machinery	....	
(5)	Interest on foreign loans	....	
(6)	Royalty, fees to foreigners	....	
(7)	Other payments for external resources	....	
(8)	*Equals:* Gross value-added to national economy		....
(9)	*Break-down into:*		
(10)	Local wages and salaries		....
(11)	Local raw materials		....
(12)	Local financial costs or interest		....
(13)	Local capital consumption (depreciation)		....
(14)	Local rental expenses		....
(15)	Other local expenses		....
(16)	Net profits		....
(17)	Total		________
(18)	Profit belonging to foreign share-holders		....
(19) = (8) - (18)	Net contribution to national economy		....
(20)	Estimated tax exemption to investors[b]		....
(21) =(19) - (20)	Merit ratio or ratio of contribution to tax exemption		....

Source: Board of Investment Memo, Thailand, May 26, 1967.

[a]Assuming operation at 80 percent of total capacity.

[b]Tax exemption on fixed assets should be amortized for the period of their useful life or the period used for the computation of depreciation.

are required to open up the possibility of national capital participation, following a specified period and in proportions to be specified by the government. The government may require commitment to a training program whereby technical and managerial skills may be acquired by Indonesians over a specified period of time; likewise, it may require the increased utilization of local resources and a positive balance-of-payments effect. The awarding of incentives is linked to (1) exceeding a minimum scale of foreign investment, (2) essentialness of product, (3) speed of start-up time, (4) location of production facilities, and (5) initial ownership structure. The problems associated with the system are really twofold: (1) the vulnerability of official decisions to personal ties and favors, and (2) the lack of authority in the part of the Foreign Investment Committee, which negotiates the entry conditions with foreign business. It would appear that even after agreement has been reached between the committee and a foreign firm, various of the ministries (particularly Finance), reserve the right to alter conditions, thought they are rarely of a critically important nature. It would seem that the Indonesian government does not look upon an approval of a Form B proposal as a binding contract on its side. One is told that these approved agreements sometimes contain a commitment to refer disputes to the World Bank's Centre for the Resolution of Investment Disputes. Thus far, however, no firm has attempted to force the Indonesian government to live up to its side of the bargain, apparently because no essential conditions have been unilaterally breached by the government.

The need to negotiate in new terms is reflected in the recent case of a U. S. firm whose Form B proposal was approved by the committee, but in a much revised form. The project was to have been a 60-40, U. S.-Indonesian joint venture to manufacture a consumer product. The principal problem was a tax holiday to which the firm had felt entitled which had been rejected, and a proposed license fee cut back to what the firm felt to be an unduly low percentage. What the firm had not done in its Form B, or annexed documents, was (1) to relate the cost of the tax holiday (to Indonesia) to the benefits expected to accrue therefrom, (2) to create a presumption in favor of the tax holiday's being a condition for an investment (e. g., a financial statement with and without the tax holiday), (3) to relate the license fee to a flow of benefits to which some objectively-derived dollar figure could be attached, (4) to establish a time schedule for the spin-off of U. S. ownership, a plan for accomplishing the spin-off, and the nature of the continuing relationship of the U. S. firm, after the spin-off, to assure a reliable operation on a continuing basis, (5) to demonstrate that an Indonesian tax holiday would not simply increase the tax revenues of the U. S. government at the expense of Indonesia—now or in the future, (6) to show that it is unlikely that anyone else could manufacture the same products on terms more favorable to Indonesia, and (7) to estimate the external employment, income, and welfare effect of the proposed operation. Past generation managers are not accustomed to negotiating in such terms.

That the restrictive nature of the Indonesian law has not prevented a significant level of foreign investment is indicated by the fact that between 1967 and September 1971 approvals were issued amounting to $1.6 billion.[2]

The Philippines

Some years ago the Philippines attempted to set up a rating system for foreign investment. The factors recognized were the net value-added effect and the balance-of-payments effect, modified by automatic ratings for intermediate and essential products. Conceptually, there was much wrong with the approach—such as the one-shot nature of the calculations, the weightings used, the discontinuity of the scale, the assumption of arbitrarily-selected minimum values. The screening was done by the Central Bank to determine which foreign investors should enjoy repatriation guarantees, and to what extent, but not to determine entry.

More recently, in 1968, the Philippine government limited the application of a long list of investment incentives, including project repatriation guarantees, to "preferred industries" (in which foreign ownership is limited to 40 percent), and to the higher-risk "pioneer industries." In the latter case, 100 percent foreign ownership is permitted initially, but shares must be listed on the Philippine exchange by the tenth year, and at least 60 percent spun off to Philippine owners by the end of the 20th year, unless an exception is granted. The government reserves the right at any time to step in with its own resources to ensure 60 percent Philippine ownership. A "pioneer" enterprise normally enjoys many incentives.

It would appear that the nature of the negotiation with the Philippine government is essentially of the same nature as that in Indonesia, and, as in Indonesia, tends to be subverted by personal ties and favors. (The so-called "parity" clause of the Philippine Constitution bestows on U. S. citizens equal rights with Philippine citizens in all business activities, thus exempting 100 percent U. S.-owned corporations from these restrictions, but the clause is unlikely to be extended beyond 1974.)

The Andean Pact Agreement (Colombia, Peru, Chile, Ecuador, Bolivia)

Decision No. 24 of the Andean Commission, promulgated in December 1970, specified that the member states had agreed to the establishment of fixed standards for foreign investment and licensing. The purpose was to prevent competition among the member states in terms of investment incentives, to further the integration of the five economies, to strengthen national enterprise (that owned at least 80 percent by the nationals of the five countries), to give national enterprises greater access to modern technology, and to give certain assurances to foreign investors and contractors. Although entry permits are given to foreign investors by the five governments, the latter agreed that certain conditions should be enforced; specifically,

1) that foreign direct investment shall not be permitted in activities considered inadequately developed by existing enterprises;
2) that foreign direct investors shall not be permitted to acquire existing national enterprises except in the case of bankruptcy (in which case up to 50 percent of the equity of the enterprise must be offered for sale to national investors within 15 years);
3) that foreign participation in national or mixed enterprises (those 51 to 80 percent owned by Andean nationals, or 50 percent or less, if the

government is participating and has a decisive capacity in decision making) may be authorized so long as the investment represents an increase in capital and does not change the character of the enterprise (that is, from national to mixed);

4) that tariff or quota preferences among the Andean countries shall only be made available to national and mixed enterprises, or to foreign enterprises undergoing transfer into national or mixed concerns. (Foreign enterprises as of July 1, 1972, have three years to advise their host government as to their intention to become either national or mixed, in which case they may benefit from the quota and tariff preference system.);
5) that any foreign investor commit himself to sell the stock he requires in a new enterprise to national investors (any citizen of the five countries), within 15 years in Colombia, Chile, and Peru, and within 20 years in Bolivia and Ecuador. (The entry agreement establishes the rate of spin-off, the manner of establishing value, and the system of transfer.);
6) that foreign enterprises (those more than 50 percent foreign-owned), will have access locally to short-term credit only;
7) that no new direct foreign investment be permitted in the areas of public utilities, financial institutions, or domestic transport or communication, and that existing foreign enterprises in these fields must offer at least 80 percent of their stock for sale to local nationals within three years;
8) that contracts for the exploitation of minerals or forestry resources be limited to twenty years;
9) that, in respect to technical assistance, patent and trademark contracts, there shall be no tie-in provisions, no resale price maintenance, no production restrictions, no cross-licensing obligations, no royalties paid on unused rights, no prohibitions to export or sell a product manufactured under such contracts.

A study of the "fade-out joint ventures," with specific reference to the Andean countries, was made by Guy B. Meeker in 1970.[3] Sixty-four U. S. companies responded to his inquiry, of which 36 percent reported that the fade-out principle was acceptable to them. But of the 64 percent which rejected the idea, 54 percent reported that they did accept minority positions in joint ventures, and 18 percent of those rejecting the minority positions indicated that they would accept the fade-out. Therefore, Meeker concluded that perhaps 70 percent of the firms studied were candidates for fade-out arrangements "if the conditions and circumstances bearing on the situation were sufficient to warrant such a decision."[4] In fact, 20 percent of the firms responded that they felt that the fade-out joint venture had a future as a form of direct U. S. investment in Latin America because it was in Latin America's interests, 40 percent because U. S. business would probably accept it.[5] Over 52 percent of these respondents indicated that fade-out offered a "worthwhile means of reducing political uncertainty," and nearly all suggested that they would cooperate, in that they would not let technology transfer lag or operations run down, or even follow a policy of minimum reinvestment–particularly if permitted to retain a minority interest.[6]

A Harvard Business School survey of 20 North American Corporations,[7] all within *Fortune's* 500, and almost all having investments in the Andean countries as well as elsewhere in Latin America, generated the finding that all but one of the companies included in the survey reported that they could live with the joint-venture relationship if required to do so. More specifically,

> It seems most apparent that although American business is unhappy with a number of the provisions of the Decision 24, no major shift of present investments is likely to occur. A majority of the companies interviewed feel the Decision per se will also not alter their future plans for their Andean investment, though a wait and see attitude was evident. It is interesting to note that the tone of most executives was one of "reacting" to the new regulations, rather than "acting" upon the new opportunities envisioned by the Pact formulators. The size of the new market was not recognized by most to be of particular significance in their investment decisions.
>
> If there is an opportunity to make a reasonable return on their investment, the Decision will not deter future funds flows. The doubts regarding the investment climate stem more from the political instability of individual countries of the region (e. g., with the uncertainties of the path Allende will follow in Chile and Peru's new industrial law) than from the Decision's provision. If #24 eventually strengthens the economic stability and reduces uncertainty of unilateral government decisions regarding investments, the Decision could conceivably be beneficial to foreign investment. Most of the executives interviewed, however, believe that the Decision will never be strictly and consistently enforced.[8]

It would appear that a growing number of countries are articulating the conditions for foreign business entry and for identifying those meriting benefits. In addition, ceilings are being placed on foreign participation by many governments.

Japan rarely permits over 50 percent foreign ownership. Yugoslavia does not permit over 49 percent foreign participation, nor do Mexico or Turkey. The Philippines, Thailand, and Taiwan have created pressures in the form of incentives pushing in the direction of increased local ownership. Indonesia bars firms, more than 49 percent foreign-owned, from engaging in importing, exporting, local distribution, and trade related services. Venezuela has adopted the 49 percent rule for the petrochemical industry. Legally required ownership sharing (with employees), such as under the recent Peruvian law, forces an eventual spin-off of some foreign ownership. In the Peruvian case, that law requires that a certain percent of pretax profit, which is otherwise considered a part of the workers' wages, are invested in a trust which purchases stock in the company in an amount of at least 50 percent. Other countries, such as Indonesia and the Andean states, impose a time limit on foreign majority ownership.

These restrictions set up several new requirements for the foreign firm; specifically,

1) the need to negotiate what is essentially an "entry contract" with the host government;
2) the need to justify a firm's activities and strategies periodically, in terms of the priorities established by the host country;
3) the need to employ individuals skilled in analyzing the impact of any enterprise on a national economy;
4) the need to maintain flexible policies with respect to ownership control, and, generally, the transfer of the resources;
5) the need to employ expatriate managers skilled in training local understudies to take over their respective jobs, which implies an incentive system to push in this direction.

Research Directions

Having thus identified what seems likely to constitute an important problem area for the international manager, one may suggest several inquiries for which research might be of special value.

I. Pressures Generating These Restricted Entry Policies

A. Questions:
1) To what extent has the Japanese "model" influenced less developed countries?
2) To what extent does the experience of one country with restrictive entry conditions (e. g., Indonesia) influence other countries to move in the same direction (e. g., the Andean group)?
3) To what extent have the policies followed by foreign-owned enterprises in these countries been responsible for the increasingly restrictive entry conditions?

B. Methodology:
1) In-depth interviews with decision makers and administrators in a sample of less developed countries; specifically to test
a) knowledge of, and response to, the Japanese model;
b) knowledge of, and response to, other LDCs with restrictive entry policies (and what are the channels of communication?) ;
c) the perceived viability of specific foreign-owned enterprises, if

they had pursued different policies and practices in the past (that is, would adherence to other policies or practices have made any difference?)

2) An examination of the entry/screening criteria being used (see Section II below) to ascertain the extent to which they have been borrowed or developed independently. (How are they justified?)

II. Identification of the Actual Entry Criteria Used

A. Questions:

1) What is the priority ordering of criteria actually used by various foreign investment contract screening bodies and why? (How specific is this ordering and the justification for it?)
2) To what extent do these criteria differ from those used by other LDC's?
3) To what extent are objective measures used?
4) In considering proposals, what time horizon is used over which absolute cut-off values are established? (That is, a screening body does not have all possible projects within its horizon at any given time. How long does it wait in establishing a preference for certain projects over others? In so doing, an absolute cut-off in terms of acceptable conditions imposed by the foreign investor/contractor is implied.)

B. Methodology:

1) Interview of screening authorities in a selected sample of LDC's.
2) Examination of a sample of accepted and rejected proposals drawn from different time periods for each country in the sample of LDCs.

III. The Quality of Negotiation

A. Questions:

1) How sophisticated and honest are government negotiators or screeners of investment/contract proposals in selecting proposals for acceptance and/or the award of special benefit?
2) How sophisticated and honest are foreign applicants in analyzing the impact of their respective proposals on those aspects of the host country environment perceived as important by the government negotiators or screeners?

B. Methodology:

1) A comparison of the answers to Questions 1, 2, 3 and 4 under II above, as derived under Methodology 1) and 2). (Does the record jibe with articulated criteria?)
2) A comparison of the answers derived under II above with more

objectively-determined measures of the criteria which screeners claim to be using and/or actually are using (if there is a difference).

3) An objective measure of the level of expertise embodied in government negotiators/screeners (e. g., advanced degrees, technical experience, use of consultants, use of models).
4) A comparison of the content of company proposals, and their justification, with the answers generated under II above.
5) In-depth interviewing of company negotiators and project writers based on a sample of firms submitting rejected proposals (another sample submitting accepted proposals).
6) A comparison of the content of company proposals, and their justification, with the answers generated under 2) above.
7) An objective measure of the level of expertise embodied in company project writers and negotiators (e. g., advanced degrees, area expertise, use of consultants, research into those questions posed under II above).

IV. Rectification of Shortcomings

A. Questions:

1) If serious deficiency is indicated in the criteria being used by LDC governments (given their own explicit objectives), or in the level of sophistication and honesty of government negotiators/screeners, what measures can be taken?
2) Same question in respect to company negotiators and project writers?

B. Methodology–general exploration with government official and company executives. Possible programs:

1) Formal training.
2) Employment of consultants to provide models.

[In each case–if answers generated under I above (i. e., pressures generating these restricted entry policies) suggest the importance of external models and past behavior–an emphasis should be placed on the uniqueness of each country in respect to location, market size, and factor endowment; on the uniqueness of each firm in respect to capabilities, resources, acceptable strategies; and, on the shift in perceptions and behavior of both host country and alien corporation overtime.]

Chapter Six

The External Affairs Function in American Multinational Corporations

J. Boddewyn

Like man, business corporations do not live by "bread" alone, since their survival does not depend only on good management within the organization and on satisfactory business performance in the marketplace. Ultimately, they must also obtain and retain the support of society and its agents, and stop them from unduly restraining their operations by means of taxation, regulation, expropriation, and/or censure. These are the positive and defensive tasks of the "external affairs" (EA) function, and they apply equally, if not more, to multinational enterprises (MNEs).

Yet, this function has been poorly researched, partly because of the low reputation of "public relations" to which it is related, and also because there is some prejudice in both the business and business-school communities against acknowledging that EA matters and can be very profitable. Thus, the prevailing ideology stresses the belief that business firms should make money through good internal management and fine performance in the marketplace, and it downplays such activities as public-relations campaigns, legislative lobbying, pressuring the executive government, and even legal action, although it is evident that protectionist laws, government subsidies, out-of-court settlements, and press campaigns are frequently necessary to protect a firm and/or foster its fortune.

Of course, political scientists have long studied *interest groups* and the role of business in influencing legislation, regulatory commissions, and various executive-government decisions. However, these studies are usually more concerned about how government action and public sentiment have been affected than about company organization for achieving such effects.[1] On its part, *social-science organizational analysis* has concerned itself with topics related to external affairs in the context of interorganizational relationships (e. g., Parsons, Evan, Thompson) and the rapport between firms and their environment.[2] Although these studies typically deal with market relations among firms, there are also analyses of community relations—particularly in the context of environmental (pollution) problems.

Of course, some parts of the international business literature deal with external affairs. The numerous "issue" studies (e. g., Behrman, Fayerweather, Kindleberger, Robinson, and Vernon) deal with the problematic matters of national interest, national sovereignty, and nationalistic feelings in the relations between multinational enterprises and host/home governments. This literature provides an analysis of the background stimuli that have led MNEs to organize themselves for external affairs. There are also *case studies* of negotiations with foreign governments, and they provide some discussion of organization structure for dealing with governments, although no in-depth analysis or survey material.[3] Equally relevant is the *international public relations literature,* even though it focuses more on mass communications than personal dealings.[4] One might also mention the various publications of Robock, Stobaugh, Root, and Nehrt dealing with the assessment of political risks; but most germane are various comments by Behrman in his three major books, and an analysis by Kapoor.[5]

The recent bibliography by Burtis and others[6] makes it evident that many publications touch upon the topic of external affairs in many ways, even though the *organization of that function within multinational enterprises* receives scant attention—but that is the very purpose of my own research.

In 1969 I started a study of the external affairs of American MNEs under the sponsorship, and with the financial assistance, of the American Management Association, which has now published the facts and conclusions gathered by Ashok Kapoor and me.[7] My research has dealt mostly with Western Europe, where I interviewed some 200 MNE executives at national and regional (i. e., Europe-wide) levels, host-government officials, U. S. embassy personnel, and various intermediaries (lawyers, bankers, American Chambers of Commerce, public relations people, etc.) in Sweden, Belgium, France, the United Kingdom, West Germany, Italy, and Switzerland in 1969-1971. My particular focus has been upon the organization of the EA function. The following sections present the highlights of my research to date and my suggestions for further development of the field.

EXTERNAL AFFAIRS GOES INTERNATIONAL

Specifically, external affairs deals with (1) government in its multiple roles as legitimizer, regulator, promoter, competitor, partner, supplier, and customer; (2) the trade-union movement as a countervailing power group; (3) trade and professional associations, as well as the rest of the industry in its noneconomic roles; (4) the intellectual, moral, and scientific communities; and (5) public opinion at large, including the potential employees, stockholders, suppliers, bankers, etc., that must be convinced of the value of offering their services to the company. Altogether, these various collectivities constitute the "nonmarket" and "macro-managerial" environments of business, that are distinct from the relatively free "markets" for the firm's inputs and outputs, and from its internal "micro-management." Hence, *external affairs is that function of the firm concerned with enlisting the support and/or negating the opposition of those nonmarket and macro-managerial collectivities that actually or potentially affect its existence and prosperity.*

In a way, all firms engage in such external affairs, be it only in the form of some deliberate or implicit "low profile," The EA function, however, is on the upswing again within the United States because of agitation about consumer and environmental protection, and of disenchantment with business in general. A growing number of American multinational enterprises are now following suit abroad.

The most obvious explanation for this recent emergence is that EA represents a countermove to the attack upon MNEs as their number, size, impact, and visibility grow. These developments bother many national governments, firms, unions, and others who feel challenged by the MNE's relative power and independence, particularly in the context of resurgent nationalism.[8] Firms then must defend themselves against various criticisms (real, false, or exaggerated) and reactions (regulations, expropriations, strikes, boycotts, etc.).

Abroad, business has long been challenged by socialistic, nationalistic, cooperativistic, and other schemes. The MNE is, thus, even more under siege than the purely domestic firm; and it must be particularly careful to make its contributions to the respective national interests evident, to minimize the impact of conflicts of sovereignties, and to avoid any clash with nationalistic feelings. It is the very matter of acquiring legitimacy that is at stake, and this is normally more difficult for a foreign body to achieve.

Besides, the problems of the parent company increasingly follow its traveling children. Thus, U. S. subsidiaries abroad have been bombed as a protest against their war-related activities in the United States; and pollution problems at home now quickly lead to inquiries about similar problems overseas.

Yet, external affairs abroad do not simply mirror the level of involvement at home because, in many cases, *more EA is needed outside the United States* because foreign governments, by and large, play a more active role in their own economy than is the case within the United States. If nothing else, this calls for a good deal of defensive action on the part of the MNE. Beyond that, however, foreign governments often encourage close relationships between the state and business in the context of economic forecasting and planning, industrial policy, regional development, and other matters. Positive action is thus indicated, too, because such association with government creates various opportunities to influence government policy and action.

Moreover, there is often more collective action abroad among business firms through cartels and trade associations, and among business, labor, and other interest groups (possibly under government auspices, as is the case in French planning). Such involvements in collective action are sometimes mandatory and often highly desirable; and the American subsidiary has to fit itself into such a "corporativistic" milieu through various EA activities.

Internal factors also influence the degree of involvement of a MNE in external affairs.[9] Company *tradition and policy* are important here, because firms range from those with no significant U. S. experience in this field or with a preference for a "low profile," to those like IBM World Trade Corporation and its subsidiaries that deliberately cover practically all their EA angles.

Size and growth are also relevant, because larger firms are more visible, and more is expected of them. Besides, expansion in other countries usually requires an explanation to other host societies that wonder why they were not chosen.

Finally, *crises* (e. g., a badly handled case of pollution) *and/or the errors of other MNEs* often precipitate involvement in external affairs or the development of that function. In a related vein, intense and successful EA activities by a competitor also make firms wonder if they are missing out on a good thing. Hence, EA staffs are emerging for a variety of reasons, whose cumulative effect is to increase awareness of the need for such an apparatus, as well as to accelerate its development. Line executives are also coming to realize that EA deserves top-management attention.

EXTERNAL AFFAIRS: LINE AND STAFF

The Role of Line Executives

A significant number of MNEs now have EA staffs at the world, regional, national and even local levels. Yet part of the function *cannot* be delegated to staff people, consultants, or even to lower-level executives, but must be handled by line people at the very top. The main reason for this situation is that the acquisition of legitimacy and community support must be handled by those who represent the "corporation" to the outside world. Another more practical reason why external affairs cannot be delegated downward is that "only real power can face power" in important negotiations and deliberations with government and other groups. Staffs and lower-level managers can, obviously, prepare the grounds and carry out routine or less crucial transactions, but only the man or men who know the total firm and control its resources can speak with full authority when important matters are at stake. This requirement is reinforced by the fact that in European countries, there is a long tradition of centralized authority whereby companies speak only through their top executive. Having a lesser executive represent the company in major external matters is interpreted as a slur upon the other partner.[10]

The Role of Staff

When the factors which condition the relative importance of the EA function rate low (e. g., size, tradition, or involvement with government), there is usually no staff. Another element favoring a small staff, or no staff at all, is that part of this function is carried out by other people and units within and outside the firm. Clearly, this diffusion calls for coordination and common servicing, but the fact remains that all external affairs do not have to be handled by a specialized internal staff. An additional shortcut consists of using the EA services of a "big sister" company. This approach is common in the petrochemicals field, wherein the petroleum company is considered to be the EA expert, or when one subsidiary is designated as the "senior company" in a particular country (see below). Some joint ventures abroad also use the EA expertise of the local partner. Furthermore, some EA activity is built into other measures such as the appointment of a local manager or the act of entering into joint ventures with local partners. Such very important ways of acquiring legitimacy do not require any EA staff—only the appropriate EA mentality.

Besides, companies can avail themselves of the external services of banks, law and CPA firms (domestic and international), public relations consultants, trade associations, American and local Chambers of Commerce, and U. S. embassies, all of which can provide information, advice, and/or introductions, or may even carry out certain negotiations for the firm.

Still, a sizeable number of firms do have an EA staff, although not necessarily at all levels, since the major problems, interest, and resources may be present only at the local, national, regional, and/or world level, and because some level (e. g., the region), may be the most appropriate one for handling external affairs and for educating the rest of the organization. Increasingly, such EA staffs report directly to the chief executive, although some firms are in the process of upgrading their public relations function, which has typically been handled at a lower level within the marketing or personnel division. Companies may thus have two staffs: (1) one more oriented toward scanning the environment and planning the appropriate moves, besides conducting some of the EA field work; and (2) another more technically oriented toward the production and release of various communications. The trend is clearly toward merging the second one into the first.

The creation of a high-level staff immediately creates the classical problems of determining the proper lines of communications with lower-level line executives, and lower-level EA staffs. The overwhelming pattern here appears to be one of "advising" ("pure" staff function), rather than of "functional" control.

EA Organization Structures

Organization structures for external affairs can be classified as minimal, intermediate, and advanced, plus a few special patterns.

Minimal Pattern

The majority of American subsidiaries in Europe at this time have only minor EA problems and deal with them on an ad hoc basis. There can be many reasons for this situation, including the ostrich-like attitude of refusing to acknowledge and face real problems. However, the major ones appear to be of small size (which facilitates a low-profile strategy), youth of investment (conducive to a "honeymoon" period), and lack of parent-company tradition and experience. Typically, then, there is no EA staff at the national and regional levels, or even in the parent company, aside from some public-relations capability. Whatever needs to be done is handled by a general manager, some appropriate subordinate (e. g., the firm's legal counsel or the financial director), or someone with "good connections" on the board of directors, or elsewhere. Actually, part of the staff may have been hired, in part or whole, precisely because of their outside connections. Banks, legal, and CPA firms, and regional development boards concerned with attracting and retaining American investors are also used; and some subsidiaries rely on a local partner or a "big sister" company to help them when necessary.

Intermediate Pattern

The minimal pattern works well until growth, age and/or crises force the subsidiary to evolve a pattern which is more explicit and more permanent. This starts a transitional phase, which is also brought about by the perception that all is not well in the world of business in general, and of the MNE in particular, and that competitors are active and apparently sucessful in external affairs. Consequently, a significant number of MNEs are going through such a reappraisal abroad and at home—a movement which can be spearheaded by a variety of people at different levels and locations. The outcome of such soul-searching is usually the development of some external-relations capability somewhere in the total organization, which, by then, has a number of subsidiaries in at least one region, and whose foreign units have acquired some surface and visibility.

The Role of the Regional Headquarters. Particularly noteworthy is the significant role of the regional (i. e., European-wide) headquarters in external affairs. This emphasis upon the regional level makes a lot of sense to the extent that it represents a halfway house between the world level, which is too heterogeneous and complex, and generally lacks the commensurate international expertise (the U. S. parent company usually does not have it), and the country level, which usually does not warrant a full-time expert. It is also a good learning-and-teaching level, since it gives the MNE an opportunity to gain some perspective about the nature and, possibly, the commonality of external-affairs problems, and to educate country subsidiaries about the importance of EA and its appropriate techniques, which are developed, frequently, on the basis of pooled experiences. Besides, the presence of several subsidiaries in a single region tends to create conflicts of national sovereignties, interests, and feelings; and this requires some multinational coordination and supranational presentation. Bad news, such as withdrawal from a particular country, is often better conveyed by regional executives, or by those sent out from parent-company offices.

Developing EA capability first in the regional headquarters is also justified by the growing importance of supranational bodies, of which there are many in Europe: the European Communities, the European Free Trade Association, the Council of Europe, the General Agreement on Tariffs and Trade (GATT), the Organization for Economic Cooperation and Development (OECD), the World Health Organization, and the Food and Agriculture Organization of the United Nations. They all deal with crucial problems affecting the MNE, and the European regional headquarters is the natural vehicle for observing these institutions and keeping them informed of the MNE's views and problems.

A related reason is that national governments typically, and increasingly, keep track of what other governments are doing—now that states have assumed more responsibilities, face a corresponding number of problems, and are continuously searching for new solutions to such matters as pollution control, consumer protection, inflation restraint, and ballooning costs of social-security systems. Many problems and solutions are, thus, no longer purely "national," but rapidly acquire a "multinational" dimension which must be handled by the MNE. Since governments tend to copy governments of neighboring countries, the regional level is the most appropriate one from which to keep track of national developments that have a potential for repercussions.

The Role of National Subsidiaries. The national level remains largely underdeveloped at this intermediate stage because (1) country general managers report only superficially about EA problems and developments in their area; (2) their EA plans are correspondingly vague and not followed up by higher levels; (3) EA action tends to be "reactive" rather than "anticipative" and "influential"; (4) national developments of potential interest to other subsidiaries in neighboring countries are not systematically brought to the latter's attention; and (5) conversely, regional or even internation developments (such as budding EEC regulations), are imperfectly perceived and followed up, nor is action taken to influence the national authorities that participate in supranational negotiations. This is, of course, where the regional headquarters plays a useful education and coordination role, although the country general managers remain responsible for identifying EA problems and developments, and for initiating the appropriate responses within the country. In any case, this intermediate stage is marked by the explicit recognition of the importance of the EA function in each nation.

This stage often involves some specialization in the form of a member of the board of directors, the company lawyer (or some other appropriate manager), or a personal assistant to the general manager, who devotes part of his time to external affairs. Such people are typically local nationals who have (or are supposed to have), particularly "good" introductions to government and/or other relevant groups. At the plant level, the local manager deals mostly with "nuisances" (pollution, noise, traffic congestion, etc.), although he may loom much larger on the horizon if he is the main employer or taxpayer in the locality.

Advanced Pattern

Very few companies have reached the stage where full EA capability—both line and staff—exists at the world, regional, national, and local (community) levels, and is properly integrated throughout a multinational organization which has been sensitized to the importance of external relations. However, some petroleum, computer, pharmaceutical, and telecommunication firms are quite close to having achieved such an advanced pattern.

These are, typically, companies organized on a geographic basis, although there may be a parallel product-based structure because of diversification (e. g., petrochemicals for the oil companies) or of "conglomeration" (e. g., ITT). They have operated in many countries for a significant length of time, and this means that the restructuring of research, production and marketing facilities goes on continuously, with concomitant effects on the economies of host and home countries. Last but not least, these companies are closely tied to government because the latter is a major customer (telecommunication and computers), owner, regulator, and/or taxer (petroleum). Pharmaceutical and food MNEs are moving in the same direction because of increasing national and supranational regulation, while the chemical and automobile firms are slowly following suit because of their vast network of production facilities which are coming under increasing centralized control by the parent company, and are being streamlined—a process which always heightens EA problems with governments, unions, and local communities.

The Role of National Line Executives. Companies at the advanced stage have key executives spending anywhere from 10 to 70 percent of their time on external affairs, while focusing on four major tasks:

1) *Identifying EA problems,* indoctrinating subordinates about them, and assigning responsibility for them. Although there is usually an EA staff, the line executive is ultimately responsible for handling such problems;
2) *Gathering environmental information* through meetings with various "elites" in government, business, labor, the press, academia, etc.—either as an individual or within the context of trade associations,

major conferences, and exclusive groups. EA staffs are very useful in this context;

3) *Obtaining general support for the firm's actions* (past, present, or contemplated) from decision makers, opinion makers, and other relevant influencers. This is achieved by means of discussions (including press interviews), speeches, congressional testimonies, and letters;
4) *Negotiating with external decision makers* when only the man who symbolizes the entire organization is considered to be a valid spokesman for the firm.

Several managers can share these tasks because there are usually two or three positions that are considered "top." Besides, various firms have former politicians and bureaucrats on their boards of directors because they are of value as advisers, "door openers," and "legitimizers" of the multinational corporation. Besides, top executives from the regional and/or world levels are occasionally "flown in" to add weight to the national subsidiary's representation.

Lower-level line executives are, of course, also active in external affairs: 1) singly when lesser matters are involved and lower-level counterparts are involved; 2) in a supporting role during negotiations; or 3) in negotiating, after having been properly introduced by a top-management representative who may well reappear when the negotiations are to be concluded, the documents signed, and the ribbons cut.

The Role of the National EA Staff. This staff assists the line executives in the gathering of information, obtaining public support, and negotiating; and it engages in various activities for which the line provides policy guidelines and the necessary budget. This double function typically encompasses the following:

1) To scan and study the nonmarket environment for relevant developments, and to diffuse this information throughout the organization, besides using the organization to generate this kind of information;
2) To assist in the education of line executives and the rest of the organization in the matter of external affairs, so that managers may be able to identify EA problems and know when to re-refer them;
3) To present the corporate view to, and obtain support from, the relevant "publics" of stockholders, government, scientific and intellectual communities, the rest of their industries, public opinion, etc.);
4) To help establish personal relations between line executives and the appropriate external agents such as government officials, trade-association executives, labor leaders, and other experts;
5) To coordinate EA activities at the national level;

6) To involve the firm in various charitable and public-interest activities as a "good corporate citizen".

Generally speaking, EA directors participate in all major policy-making meetings at their level in order to present the EA viewpoint and to be immediately informed of problems and decisions requiring some EA action. It is also their responsibility to see that the EA function is properly developed, staffed, and budgeted at lower levels, although these are ultimately decisions that are taken by line executives. A firm with several plants in the same country will often have a public relations or community relations manager head under each plant manager, unless size does not warrant it, in which case the personnel manager frequently handles it.

It is well to recognize that different companies emphasize different things in their external affairs programs since they can stress: 1) *public relations* in the sense of projecting a certain "image" for the company as far as the general public is concerned, but this may also include suppliers, neighbors, customers, and stockholders; 2) *civic relations* in terms of acting as a "good neighbor" or "good corporate citizen" by taking an active part in local and national programs (e. g., hiring the handicapped, supporting or initiating public pleas for better social amenities such as parks and swimming pools, and making charitable donations); and/or 3) *government relations* in terms of keeping track of, and influencing, the public authorities.

With reference to the latter, one oil company distinguishes between 1) "public-administration" relations concerned with the day-to-day problems of obtaining licenses (to import, manufacture, and sell), authorizations to increase prices, favorable tax rulings, etc.; and 2) "political" relations in terms of forecasting the evolution of parties, coalitions, personalities, the electorate, and government policies; and developing relations of influence with actual and potential key decision makers.

Some companies also include *employee relations* under external affairs, although elsewhere they may be handled by the personnel department. Similarly, *customer relations* may come under marketing, *press relations* under advertising, and *technical (trade, professional) relations* under manufacturing. Nevertheless, such fragmented activities must still be coordinated in some fashion.

A full-fledged EA department usually includes a variety of research and "production" specialists who gather data, prepare speeches and reports, distribute materials, organize visits of the firm, make appointments, address the press, and so on. Such a full-fledged national EA staff can easily involve 20-30 people, and its budget represent .3 to 1 percent of sales. Its activities are almost entirely performed by natives of the country, although with the assistance of the regional and world headquarters and their more multinational staffs. However, a few Americans, Canadians, and Britons handle them too, but citizens of neighboring countries do not, since national antagonisms linger on in most regions where, however, some superior ability is assumed to exist or is accepted as far as Anglo-Saxons are concerned.

Companies at this advanced stage of external affairs are quite aware of the fact that "external relations begin at home" and that their first audience is their employees and stockholders. The latter are not taken for granted, because they can act as spokesmen for the company and because they wear other hats as citizen, neighbor, and consumer, which ultimately contribute to shaping public opinion and policy.

The Role of the Regional HQ. The regional headquarters has a fully developed EA staff operating along the lines detailed above under the "intermediate pattern." This staff is normally smaller than that found in the large national subsidiaries because its role is more one of assisting, coordinating, prodding, developing, and educating national staffs than of "managing" them.

Fundamentally, the Regional EA Director's job is to insure that national subsidiaries develop an appropriate awareness and capability in this field. Besides, the regional headquarters' role is often that of diligent broker among subsidiaries; and meetings of national EA directors are organized once or twice a year in order to exchange information about current problems and relevant experiences.

Besides, the Regional EA Director relays information about significant developments in the U. S., such as the progress of protectionist bills and government policy toward East-West trade; it often passes judgment on the relevance of American EA themes and materials for the region. However, some EA communications go directly from the parent company to the subsidiaries, as when certain announcements must be released quasi simultaneously all over the globe.

Still, there are some direct EA activities conducted on a regional scale. Together with the chief regional executive, the Regional EA Director participates in discussions and negotiations with national governments when a new subsidiary is about to be created, when some plants are being closed down or expansion plans curtailed, or when a particular country is bypassed during expansion into a particular region. Such representations are normally made in conjunction with the national managers in order to stress that the latter are not mere puppets.

The Role of the World HQ. This it the least developed part of external affairs. For one thing, American MNEs are only beginning to face the new challenges to their existence abroad and, now, at home. More generally, many large American companies have only recently begun to develop their external-affairs function in the face of the new (or newly discovered) problems associated with pollution, consumerism, youth, women, and other minorities. For example, the post of "International Washington representative" is a relatively new one in many firms. Furthermore, the existing EA staffs of the parent company are typically busy with American problems. Additionally, the EA function must be closely tailored to national and regional conditions. Thus, it is fairly obvious that the experience developed in Latin America or Asia is not particularly relevant to Western Europe. Finally, the men who, because of their experience and temperament, are capable of handling external affairs on a worldwide basis are very scarce. However, their number is slowly increasing. They often are foreigners because the needed relevant experience was more easily obtained abroad and because they are more skilled in the art of sensitizing the parent company to foreign problems in this area.

Thus, the embryo of a worldwide EA staff and the orientation of line executives is present and developing. More top executives in the parent companies are now returnees from overseas assignments, where they learned the importance of EA abroad. Moreover, public relations are beginning to be well handled on an international scale; the legal staff of the parent company concerns itself with U. S. implications of actions taken abroad; teams of specialists are flown overseas to participate in negotiations; home-office executives are escorted around to cultivate European elites; and regional and national subsidiaries are kept informed of major American developments.

The world headquarters of American MNEs may also be involved in monitoring the supranational agencies located in the United States—particularly, the United Nations and the International Monetary Fund. New York and Washington are excellent listening posts because of the presence of embassies and internationally-oriented associations such as the National Foreign Trade Council, the Conference Board, the Council of the Americas, and the Council on Foreign Relations.

Special Patterns

We saw earlier that regional headquarters may serve as some sort of a "big uncle" for national subsidiaries that do not have an EA staff. Another way of assisting national subsidiaries is to have one subsidiary help another within the same nation or region. Such a "big sister" arrangement usually reveals the fact that one company, because of its age, size, product line, etc., has more EA experience which is relevant for younger, smaller, and/or related subsidiaries of the same parent. The foremost example is that of the petroleum companies assisting petrochemicals companies in the same region and nation.

Another variation of this theme occurs when one product division within the firm is more experienced than others and therefore carries out the EA function for the entire company, as is the case of the national subsidiary of a very diversified firm wherein the Computer Division services the office equipment, industrial equipment, and consumer products divisions.

In the "senior officer" pattern used by very diversified firms and conglomerates, the key officer of the largest (or oldest) subsidiary assumes responsibility for the external affairs of the others. Typically, this subsidiary has more EA experience, and its senior officer, who is always a local national, carries great prestige and has excellent connections with various elites in the country. This form is also used when the subsidiaries cannot be brought readily under an "IBM-France" type of umbrella—for example, when some of the subsidiaries must look very "national" because the government is a major customer or because association with American ownership may otherwise harm the company's sales (e. g., in the field of traditional foods).

FURTHER RESEARCH

This brief review of the literature as well as the above analysis of "organizing for external affairs around the world," suggest four broad directions for further research: (1) study of additional dimensions of EA organization structures; (2) expansion of existing studies to cover more companies, countries, and regions; (3) relation of the findings of these studies to organization theory in order to interpret them and to develop further hypotheses for research; and (4) analysis of the role of intermediaries in relations between business and its external-relations environment. In particular, the following topics are presently being explored by this author, as well as various master and doctoral candidates:

1) How do firms "monitor" their external affairs (i. e., nonmarket and macro-managerial) environment at the local, national, regional, and world levels and how can this monitoring be improved in terms of structure and process?
2) What people are presently employed in EA positions? How can their selection, training, and appraisal be appraised and improved?
3) How can the role of various "international intermediaries" be appraised and improved:
    - lobbyists;
    - lawyers;
    - bankers;
    - American Chambers of Commerce abroad;
    - U. S. embassies;
    - public relations firms.
4) What is the role of the "Washington Representative" in international business-government relations?
5) What is the role of the legal counsel at the parent and subsidiary levels in international business-government relations?
6) What EA structures are developed to handle certain problems such as disinvestment, expropriations, and crises of the recent ITT-type?

7) What are the transitional and more permanent problems created for the EA function by shifts in overall organization structure (E. G., from the international-division basis to a product or geographic basis)?
8) What coordination structure is needed when the EA function is handled by a local partner?
9) What are the similarities and differences between the handling of the EA function by local companies and by U. S. subsidiaries in the same foreign countries?
10) How do foreign firms organize themselves for the EA function in the United States?
11) How can one improve the measurement of the costs and benefits of the EA function?
12) How are policies developed in this field, and what are they?

As mentioned above, the answers to such questions also must be related to the literature of organization theory (e. g., institutional and boundary roles),* and to the analyses of such topics as "strategy and structure," "organization and environment," and "multinational organization." Only then will our knowledge of "multinational organization for external affairs" match the one already developed for such matters as multinational marketing and finance.

*For a more theoretical treatment of the subject see: J. J. Bodden, Jr., "External Affairs: A Corporate Function in Search of Conceptualization and Theory" (a paper presented at the May 1973 CARI Conference, Center for Business and Economic Research, Kent State University; and to be included in the proceedings of that conference).

Chapter Seven

Government, Politics, and the Multinational Enterprise

David H. Blake

The multinational enterprise is and has good reason to be deeply concerned about the business environment fostered by host-state political systems and their governments. The gain or loss of investment incentives, the ability or inability to raise prices in the light of mandated wage increases, the existence and the nature of necessary attributes of a social and industrial infrastructure, and the ultimate question of the retention or loss of ownership and control are just a few of the myriad ways in which the political and governmental systems of a host state can affect adversely or positively the environment for conducting business. Similarly, most of the obstacles to private foreign investment in host states, as perceived by a sample of international business executives, were thought to be a function of government policies, of government administration, and of a country's political, economic, or structural environment.[1]

To a significant extent, the reduction and elimination of these barriers and the development and maintenance of a favorable environment for a multinational firm seem to be within the direct or indirect purview of host-state politics and government. In other words, the attitudes and actions of the host-state political and governmental systems are critical determinants of how multinational enterprises can conduct business, and therefore influence their objectives, actions, and procedures. It is precisely because of the state's ability to influence the corporation, and the mounting concern about direct foreign investment in host states that the multinational corporation likewise seeks to influence host-state government and politics. This latter relationship is the general topic of this chapter. However, before developing a framework within which it is useful to examine multinational enterprise attempts to influence host-state government and politics, it will be helpful first to consider the central concept of influence and then, briefly, to discuss influence conflicts resulting from host state-multinational firm interaction.[2]

INFLUENCE: THE CENTRAL CONCEPT

As has been implied, at the heart of relations between multinational firms and host states are the attempts of each to influence or control the behavior of the other. By influence attempt we mean an effort which seeks to modify the behavior of a target actor so that its actual behavior is different from what it would have been in the absence of the influence attempt. An influence attempt is successful when the desired behavioral modification is achieved. Note, though, the relational aspect of influence. Influence is not something that one party has and the other has not. Rather it is a relationship, a behavioral relationship, and the existence of influence of one over another is as dependent upon the second party as it is upon the first. If the target actor refuses to be influenced, that is, to modify his behavior, then there is little that the one who would influence can do about it. Thus, in our discussion of influence attempts between multinational corporations and host states, it is most important to keep in mind the behavioral nature of the relationship and the equally important part both parties play in this relationship.

A second aspect of the concept of influence also needs to be mentioned. Influence attempts may seek to change the behavior of an actor from one position to another, or influence attempts may seek to prevent an actor from changing his behavior from a satisfactory status quo to a less desirable new position. Thus, we can speak of influence attempts designed to *preserve* desirable behavior and influence attempts seeking to *promote* modifications in behavior.

In addition to the direct, bilateral influence relationship between two parties, the attempt to exert influence may take a more indirect circuitous route by which to obtain the desired behavior on the part of a target; the initiator of the influence attempt may have to influence an intermediate party, who will then seek the desired behavior from the eventual target. Thus, A may seek to influence C through B (Figure 7-1).

Having briefly discussed the concept of influence in conceptual terms, we will now try to indicate how it is applicable to the relationship between host states and multinational enterprises. Host states seek to utilize private foreign investment to advance various objectives of a political,

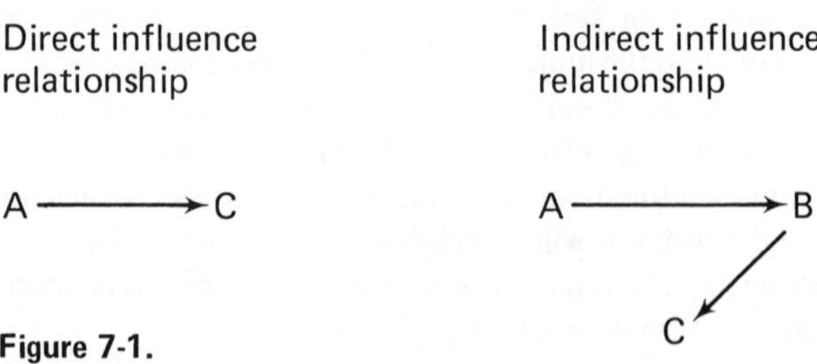

Figure 7-1.

economic, social, and cultural nature.[3] In order to achieve this, host governments have imposed requirements and regulations on multinational enterprises which force these firms to pursue certain activities which they might not have followed had they been permitted to operate in an unconstrained environment. Thus, these rules and regulations, and also many more informal devices, attempt to modify the behavior of firms towards certain goals. As was pointed out in the workshop, it is likely that host-state attempts to influence or control the behavior of multinational enterprises will grow in number, scope, and intensity.

Conversely, multinational firms also seek to modify the behavior of host states to promote changes in governmental policies or practices which would be more favorable to the interests of the foreign enterprises. Depending upon the situation, some international business firms will also attempt to influence government decision-making, so that modifications of policy which are feared will not be instituted, since the status quo is preferable to proposed policies. No doubt many companies in many states find themselves pursuing *promotive* and *preservative* influence-attempts at the same time. Indeed, it was the general consensus of the workshop that most multinational enterprises are concerned primarily with legitimizing themselves, with taking part in governmental programs and incentives, and with avoiding penalties.

Thus far, we have been concerned primarily with the bilateral influence relationship involving multinational enterprises and host governments. However, this is a rather narrow view, for the many social, economic, political, and cultural groups which participate in the political process are also concerned about the activities of multinational enterprises because of the impact of these firms. Societal groups such as political parties, labor unions, defenders of the local culture, competitors, suppliers, consumers, and many many more may wish to influence the behavior of these enterprises to conform more closely to their objectives. Such groups may seek to modify the behavior of corporations through direct pressure on the firm, through protests and demands focused on the government of the host state, or through effective utilization of the political process. The government of the host state also may attempt to influence the multinational corporation by using nongovernmental groups, such as an employers association. Using a similar strategy, the multinational enterprise itself may try to influence government policies by persuading important domestic groups to use their influence upon the government to bring about the desired changes. In other cases, the eventual targets of corporate influence-attempts are these host state nongovernmental groups, but the strategy calls for influencing, first, government policy which may then affect the practices of these groups.

Henry Ford's visit to the United Kingdom is a case in point; he attempted to influence the British government to enact new and restrictive labor legislation which would reduce the amount of labor instability and unrest, thereby making the investment climate in Great Britain more acceptable to Ford.

There is another type of intermediate actor which should be mentioned—the government of the parent company. There are numerous allegations and a number of documented instances in which the multinational enterprise has sought to influence the host-country government by use of the position and influence capability of the parent country. The well-known Calvo Doctrine, adopted by many Latin American countries, is designed to prevent this type of activity by United States-based multinational enterprises. Of course, the reverse relationship can also occur whereby a host government seeks the aid of the parent-country government to influence the behavior of a recalcitrant multinational enterprise. A number of participants in the workshop predicted that, increasingly, negotiations involving international business activities would involve host governments, parent governments, and the multinational enterprise. The active role of the parent government would be the result of its desire to protect the interests of those groups which might be harmed by the foreign investment. However, this prediction by some was firmly rejected by others who feared that tripartite sessions would be unbearably complex, long, and unnecessarily drawn-out.

The framework, or model, of the influence relationship between multinational firms and host governments described above can be usefully diagrammed as follows: "T" indicates the ultimate target of the influence attempt or the actor from which behavioral change or behavioral preservation is sought. The diagrams are symmetrical, indicating the fact that the influence relationship between host states and multinational enterprises are reciprocal, or mutual, in nature. This makes sense, for if one element seeks to influence another, then it is likely that the second element will wish to have some influence over the former. (See Figure 7-2.)

The preceding diagram merely tries to illustrate that which is already well known to the student or practitioner of international business—the host-country government, the political process, and various social, political, economic, and cultural groups seek to influence the multinational enterprise, and, conversely, the multinational firm seeks to influence these critical components of its environment. The chapters by Behrman, Fayerweather, and Robinson explore the objectives and concerns of host governments in some detail. Similarly, Fayerweather's study of host-country elite attitudes towards these firms indicates the varying concerns held by important officials of both governmental and nongovernmental types of organizations.[4]

The host government is obviously and directly involved in the behavior and impact of multinational enterprises, but there are, as illustrated, a great many more nongovernmental groups which also are interested in the activities of these firms and which may attempt to influence the behavior

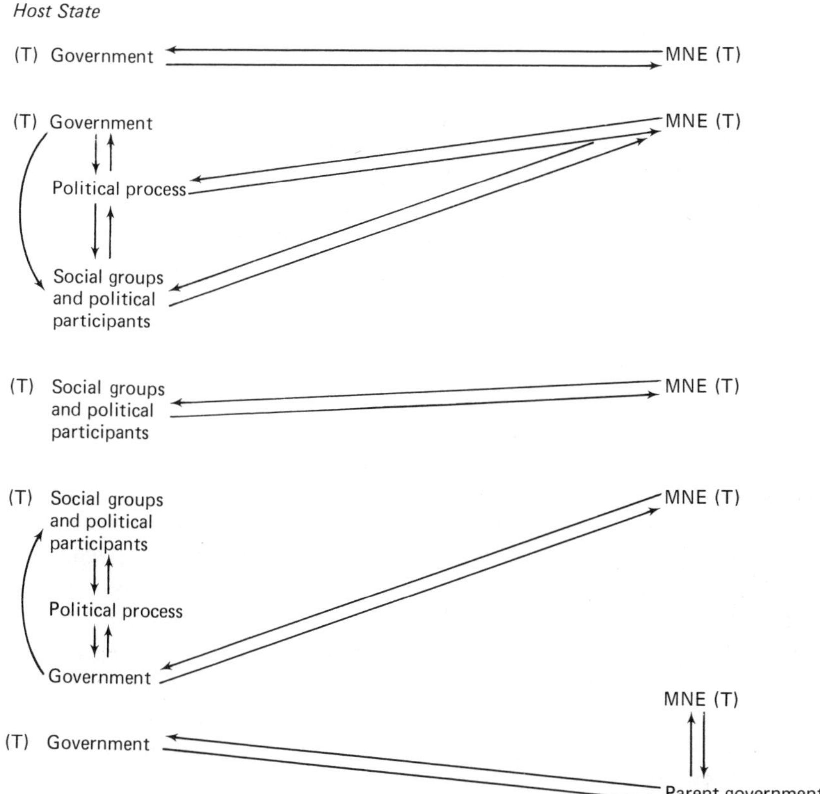

Figure 7-2. Model of the MNE = Host State Influence Relationship

Note: The lines between the various actors represent the communication system as well, and this, too, is subject to influence attempts by host states and multinational enterprises.

of the corporations. These groups will try to exert influence directly on the multinational enterprise, or they may participate in political activities which seek to influence the host government so that it will demand appropriate behavior from the firms. One category of concerned groups would be those which perceive themselves to be directly affected by the actions of the multinational corporation, and which are relatively *issue-oriented* in their concern. Labor unions, groups of competing or local supplier businessmen, community groups concerned with pollution problems, and other similar organizations attempt to influence multinational firms in a way that may result in more desirable behavior, from their viewpoints. In addition to such issue-oriented groups, multinational enterprises are faced by influence attempts deriving from *ideologically-oriented* groups, some of which seek to restrict these firms severely or, perhaps, eliminate them altogether. Whereas groups in the previous category express concern about specific ways in which they are affected by foreign firms, the ideological groups are motivated by basic questions concerning the role of foreign and capitalistic enterprises in the host state. These groups are often out to challenge the very existence and legitimacy of multinational firms, and they use direct pressure on the firm, and pressure on the political process and the government in pursuit of their objectives. This fact is frequently and conveniently neglected by academics studying host state-international business relations. Multinational enterprises are not operating in an ideological vacuum in host states, and a policy of ignoring the arguments and actions of those who seek elimination of direct foreign investment altogether may be absurd from the viewpoint of self-preservation.

Because of the importance of the political, social, economic, and governmental environment presented by host states, multinational enterprises seek to influence or shape that environment to conform more closely to their needs and desires. In his chapter, Boddewyn has explored the substance of corporate objectives pursued through external-affairs activities, but it will be useful for the current discussion to identify four different types of objectives motivating such influence attempts. First, multinational enterprises may be interested in influencing host-state politics and government concerning an issue which is specific to and which will benefit a particular corporation and its environment. The lowering of an onerous import duty on a critical component, facilitation of special government permits necessary for uninterrupted operation, and the resolution of an industrial dispute are just a few examples of situations in which a specific firm may seek to influence the local government or social groups in support of specific behavioral modifications deemed to be beneficial. Probably a majority of international business external-affairs activities are stimulated by this kind of concern.

Secondly, a multinational firm may seek to influence its environment in such a way that will benefit an entire industry, which may be composed of both local and foreign firms. Thus, an effort to obtain increased import duties on competitive products from abroad will favor all domestic manufacturers of that product regardless of origin of ownership. Similarly, requests to a government for use of its influence with workers striking against an industry will benefit all manufacturers. Thirdly, multinational enterprises may join with other international firms to influence government or society in a way which will make it easier for foreign firms to undertake operations. Certainly, the antiforeign investment provisions of the Andean Common Market have caused groups of multinational enterprises to try to reduce the stringency of these regulations. As Jack Behrman suggested in the workshop discussion, frequently United States-based multinational corporations work through the local branch of the American Chamber of Commerce to protect the interests of foreign investment, although the positive impact of such efforts appears to be doubtful.[5]

Finally, multinational corporations may join with domestic capitalistic enterprises in support of efforts to create a more favorable political, economic, social, and governmental environment for private enterprise, and capitalism in general. Thus, external affairs activities of the international business firm may be used to convey the message of the benefits accruing to society as a result of the activities of capitalism to counteract the efforts of ideological groups proclaiming a very different view. During the workshop, several members mentioned the difficulty of pursuing this tactic in Latin America because of the generally negative attitude toward capitalism. The preceding categorization of the objectives of external affairs actions will be useful, subsequently, in the discussion of multinational-enterprise attempts to influence host states, but at this point it is perhaps sufficient to identify, as the major point of distinction, the degree and nature of specificity or generality of the influence attempts.

One final point needs to be made before examining factors which affect the efforts of multinational firms to influence host states, and this involves, more specifically, the targets of these actions. Clearly, one target of such activity is the host government, its policies, its decisions, and its implementation of policies and decisions. By focusing efforts upon the government, multinational enterprises seek to influence the outcomes of government decision-making as they affect a specific firm, an industry, foreign investment in general, or private enterprise, even more generally. At other times, multinational corporations may seek to influence the political process of the host state in support of its objectives. Here the focus is not on the outcomes of government decision-making, but on the political process by which demands and supports are fed into the decision-making network. In other words, by favorably influencing or structuring the political system, the government outputs may be more positive. Another target, obviously related to the first two, involves the various societal actors, groups and individuals, who are actual or potential participants in the host-nation political process. In this case, the multinational enterprise, in pursuit of its several objectives, attempts to influence various social, political, and economic groups in a manner that will bring about desirable behavior on their part, or which, more generally, will lead to a more receptive environment for the achievement of the aims of the firm. A final target of multinational enterprise-influence attempts is the host-state communication system which conveys information and messages upon which perceptions of "reality" and, therefore, political decisions are likely to be based. In conclusion, the targets of multinational enterprise influence-attempts reflect the relationship in host countries between government, the political processes, participants in the political system, and the communication net. All four targets present important points of access for multinational firms which seek to influence the environment in host states.

MNE AND POLITICAL SYSTEMS: AN ANALYTICAL FRAMEWORK

To plan and implement efforts to influence host states, multinational enterprises need to have a clear understanding of how the host-state governmental/political system works, and then to design strategies which are appropriate for that particular state, situation, and corporation. However, this is not an easy task, for countries differ in terms of levels of development, systems of government and politics, and historical, cultural, ideological, and political traditions. Consequently, the analytical framework presented below is a general one which uses concepts and terms which allow the analyst to cut through the maze of different governmental and political institutions found in various countries, to focus on the important host-state functions and political relationships which lead to an understanding of how the system works. The framework is based on a structural-functional approach to the four targets of corporate influence-attempts—host-state government, political process, participants in the political process, and communication net.[6] This means that the analysis of these targets begins with the identification of a number of crucial functions performed in political systems and then proceeds to a discovery and analysis of those institutions or structures which actually perform these functions. While the framework is conceptual and general in presentation, it becomes pragmatic and operational upon application to a specific situation.

One function of a governmental nature which is found in all systems is the rule-making function, but the structures or institutions which actually do make the rules vary from country to country and, probably, from issue to issue. For instance, the colonels of Peru occupy a major role in making decisions about the place and nature of foreign investment in that country, but, in contrast, recent but unsuccessful efforts in the Netherlands to tax severely new foreign investment in the more industrialized portions of that state suggest a very different set of actors involved in rulemaking.

Two other governmental activities of obvious importance to the multinational enterprise are the role-application function and the rule-adjudication function. The former involves the implementation and execution of the rules agreed upon, and the latter is concerned with the determination of whether a rule has been violated, the seriousness of the infraction, and the appropriate penalty to be assessed. It is important to know, though, which institutions perform each function and the manner in which it is undertaken. Whether the same institution is involved in both the rule-application and rule-adjudication functions or entirely different structures are involved will be important for the design of influence strategies.

An alternative strategy for multinational firms seeks to affect government policies by changing the nature of the demands and pressures received by the rule-making structures by focusing on the political process or input functions of interest articulation and interest aggregation. Interest articulation involves the manner in which needs, interests, and demands are conveyed from groups and individuals in society to those performing governmental functions. In some states, the process may be rather formal and routinized, with specific rules of behavior, and might involve such things as the mass media, political parties, legislative and bureaucratic hearings, etc. However, in other states and sometimes in the same states, interest articulation may be more spontaneous and ad hoc in nature, including such actions as demonstrations and riots. Examples are France in 1968, Poland in 1970, and Chile in 1972.

Interest aggregation, a second political process function, is the process by which demands and concerns articulated are combined, collapsed, and winnowed to produce general policy alternatives which are then subject to governmental functions. How this occurs varies from political system to political system, and with the nature of the issue as well, but its importance for the development of corporate influence strategies is clear.

Regarding the participants in the political process, the two fundamental functions to be analyzed are those of political recruitment and political socialization. The former refers to the process by "which the roles of political systems are filled,"[7] and has obvious relevance for the various functions already discussed. Its usefulness as a target for international firms is most doubtful, though. However, the political socialization function, involving the process by which political participants (potential or actual) obtain values, attitudes, and beliefs about the system and political matters is a candidate for corporate influence attempts.

There is one more function which is fundamental for any political system and which may be a target or vehicle for multinational enterprise-influence attempts. This is the communication function, and it interacts with, and has relevance for, all the other functions which have already been discussed. The nature and transmission of information is the glue which binds the whole system together, and it provides the data which stimulate actions by the various functional actors.

For each of the functions discussed above, it is necessary to follow the methodology of structural-functional analysis. A first step involves the description and analysis of the various forms or styles of functional activity. While the basic function itself is identical from one state to another, precisely how it is performed does vary and may have some impact on the success or failure of multinational corporate-influence attempts. A second step requires the identification of all those structures which are engaged in the specific functional activity. Furthermore, each structure or institution should then be analyzed in terms of its nature, its composition, and its demography. Fourthly, an analysis of the dynamics of how each structure performs the relevant function is also important.

A fifth step involves conducting a structural-functional pattern analysis for each function and for the political/governmental system more generally. Specifically, this entails an effort to determine the general relationship between structures and functions. A system can be characterized by multifunctionality, wherein various structures perform a number of different functions. An extreme, but important, case of multifunctionality occurs when a single structure has a dominant role in the performance of several or more and different functions. Other systems can be characterized by functional specificity where each structure has a rather precise role to play, which is generally not shared by others. On the other hand, there exist systems of structural overlap whereby different institutions share in the performance of the same function. A structural-functional pattern analysis is necessary because it indicates the patterns of power or importance among structures, and the functional basis or bases of this power. From the perspective of the corporate analyst, this type of analysis reveals needed information for the development of a strategy which is appropriate for the specific situation of concern.

The last stage of the methodology suggested involves an identification and assessment of the nature and appropriateness of the channels available for multinational enterprise influence attempts. What are the appropriate channels for influence activity with respect to specific functions and structures? Are they sufficiently well developed for corporate influence-efforts, and are they open to such attempts? Are the channels so clogged with other claimants that it is appropriate for the firm to use and develop other existing but little used channels? Or is multinational corporate activity in a particular area considered to be illegitimate? These and similar questions about the channels for influence efforts must be considered before embarking upon a particular influence strategy.

Essentially, this is a scheme by which an analyst can separate a complex governmental/political system into its critical processes or functions, and its relevant structures. By following the procedure presented, the various points of access for influence efforts and their relationship to the overall system are highlighted. Combining this framework with the propositional framework discussed later should, at least, alert the external-affairs officer to the opportunities and potential problems associated with a particular influence effort. Neither framework gives the answers to questions confronting concerned executives or scholars, but they do provide a methodology for planning and implementing strategies.

MNE INFLUENCE ATTEMPTS: SOME PROBLEMS AND RECOMMENDATIONS

Having presented a methodology by which one can analyze the nature of a state's political/governmental system from the vantage point of corporate influence-attempts, we can now examine some of the particular problems faced by multinational corporations in these endeavors which, frequently, are not important for domestic enterprises. The "foreignness" of the multinational enterprise produces rather fundamental problems when it tries to influence the environment of the host-state political system. Unlike the domestic enterprise, the international firm is not considered to have the same values, attitudes, commitments, and identity with the host state that a domestic firm would have. These difficulties are compounded by the fact that multinational firms vary significantly in the nature and degree of their foreignness and their dependence upon the host-state envornment.

There are, of course, many different schemes which have been developed to classify types of multinational enterprisee, but Howard Perlmutter's threefold classification is appropriate for this point.[8] An ethnocentric firm is a completely foreign entity. Corporate ownership, control, objectives, standards, and top-management personnel are all foreign in nature, or have an essentially foreign reference point. The actions of the firm are basically those of a foreign actor. In contrast, the geocentric enterprise is international in ownership, management, objectives, and standards. While this type of firm may have discarded its foreign-state orientation, it is still a foreign actor, albeit an international one, from the point of view of the host-state political system. The locus of power, decision making, and the setting of standards for performance are beyond the scope of the host state. In both the ethnocentric and geocentric cases, the subsidiaries are clearly foreign enterprises, and while successful operations need a favorable host-state environment, the orientation is foreign.

Subsidiaries which have the characteristics of polycentric firms are much more dependent upon the local environment. Although owned by foreigners, such firms are, in most other respects, very much like local enterprises. The management, often of host-state origin, is left relatively free to develop and implement its own objectives and strategies to service the domestic market. Since a polycentric subsidiary is a rather self-sufficient entity, with respect to the rest of the operations of the international corporation and is largely independent of its headquarters, it succeeds or fails according to its ability to conduct business in the host-state environment. In spite of these basically local characteristics, this type of subsidiary, like the other two, usually lacks full acceptance as a participant in the host-state political system and process. Even though it is deeply concerned with the nature of its environment in the host state, and differs little from a local firm, its actions regarding the shaping of that environment are often suspect, and generally are very carefully observed by other actors in the political process.

Several other general characteristics of the multinational corporation, in contrast to the domestic firm, are also important for corporate influence-attempts. The foreignness of the firm frequently is associated with and exacerbates concern about giant size and significant power. Even though an international firm may not be large and powerful, host-state actors will be quick to play upon the fears and suspicions aroused by the actions of, not only a foreign entity, but also a large and powerful one. Evidence of this kind of activity can be found in the frequent comparisons of sales revenues of major United States-based multinational corporations and the national budgets or gross national products of selected states. These comparisons are obviously meaningless, but do provide sensational examples of the size and power of such firms. This type of strategy is used to question the legitimacy or appropriateness of multinational enterprise influence-attempts.

The preceding sentences also suggest another factor, previously mentioned, which hinders efforts to influence the environment. There are both issue-oriented and ideologically-motivated groups in the host state which find it in their best interests to provoke or promote the fears of other domestic groups of the potential evils and excesses of multinational enterprises. This means, of course, that the international firm has competitors of a political sort, who will try to make it difficult for those firms to participate actively and sensitively in the political/governmental system.

There are a number of implications to be drawn from these factors for multinational enterprise influence-attempts. In seeking to affect government policy through the role-making, rule-application, and rule-adjudication functions, multinational enterprises should probably concentrate their efforts on the formal influence channels which provide access to the structures which perform these tasks. To the extent that such channels do exist and by which various concerned interests can legitimately seek to influence government-type actions, the international corporation should use them, but at the same time, it needs to avoid the semblance of applying too much pressure on the targets of influence actions. If it does not, various competing interests may cloak themselves in the righteousness of nationalism to try to prevent that firm from achieving its goals. The utilization of employers groups and other similar associations may allow the foreign firm to pursue its own interests in concert with numbers of domestic units seeking the same type of environment.

The multinational enterprise should probably avoid the use of informal influence channels, particularly when publicity regarding such efforts would cause embarrassment to the firm or to the targets of its activity. It may be appropriate for domestic corporations to seek to influence governmental functional actors in this way, but the attributes of foreignness, size, and power suggest that a similar strategy for the multinational enterprise would be ill advised. This is particularly so, given the fact that there are competitors anxious to point out the indescretions of foreign firms. However, in some countries where the formal mechanisms for influencing governmental policy are underdeveloped or nonexistent, the multinational corporation may be forced to use informal channels or may find it necessary to create new channels for influence attempts. In either case, however, the influence effort should be conducted openly and sensitively, so that undue concern is not aroused by a combination of secretiveness and foreignness.

With respect to the attempt to exert influence through the political process functions, the multinational enterprise should again seek to use the formal and routinized channels of interest articulation and interest aggregation. However, the international firm must be most careful to avoid becoming involved in partisan political activity. The public and non-threatening use of channels for interest representation is acceptable, but, unlike domestic firms, the foreign enterprise has no role whatsoever in the struggles of domestic political conflict.

Similarly, the search for influence through the recruitment function is unwise from the point of view of corporate policy. Expatriate and domestic managerial personnel should be prohibited from becoming involved in the selection process, even though in some states domestic economic enterprises take a very active role in the recruitment function. However, there is no justification for activity by foreigners in this area.

There are some opportunities for multinational firms to become involved in the socialization function. The creation of an awareness of the contribution of the firm and the type of environment necessary for continuation of such efforts is certainly within the province of influence activity. Since individuals—office holders, potential office-holders, political activists, and potential political-activists—learn about politics and the political culture through the socialization function, it is a reasonable but, perhaps, long-range influence strategy for multinational enterprises to engage in advertising, employee programs, public and community relations, and similar activities with the objective of creating a more favorable environment. Rather than a wide-ranging effort at socialization, which may cause resentment and resistance, the international enterprise should focus its efforts on those domestic groups with which it has frequent and legitimate contacts—such as employees, consumers, suppliers, and people in the immediate community. Here again, though, these efforts ought not to be heavy-handed and overwhelming, giving the impression that the full weight of the entire firm, including its international headquarters, is being brought to bear on this activity.

Attempts to influence the host environment through the

communication function should, also, be carefully considered. In some cases, access may be gained quite easily, and such efforts may be pursued judiciously, but, again, the important qualifiers of moderation, sensitivity, and awareness of one's foreignness are recommended.

In summation, with respect to attempts to influence the environment, the multinational corporation differs from the domestic corporation in that it is foreign, it is thought to be large and powerful, and it has a number of competitors who will not hesitate to rely upon the arguments of nationalism and foreign intervention to thwart any influence efforts. These differences mean that the multinational enterprise, in addition to basing its strategies and actions upon the goals, values, and standards of the host state, must try to conduct itself in a public and open fashion when seeking to influence its environment. The content of such thrusts should be exhibited as advancement of the interests of the host state, and the style should reflect sensitivity to the fears and suspicions of foreign entities. Efforts suggesting secrecy, overwhelming power, partisan politics, or reliance upon foreign sources of strength must be avoided. Furthermore, multinational corporate influence-attempts are probably best pursued through the formal channels of access to the governmental functional actors and, if they exist, to the structures involved in interest articulation and aggregation. The socialization and communication functions are also potentially important for long-range efforts. However, because of its particularly vulnerable position, the multinational enterprise should, generally, seek to be an even better corporate citizen than its domestic counterpart.

MNE AND POLITICAL SYSTEMS: A PROPOSITIONAL FRAMEWORK

Keeping in mind the various characteristics of influence, the different types of objectives and targets involved, and the analytical framework just presented, it is now possible to examine several variables which may affect the success or failure of corporate attempts to influence host states. In undertaking a discussion of this relationship, one must be careful not to be so general as to lose any chance of applicability to specific cases, while avoiding a degree of specificity from which it is most difficult to generalize. There may not be a satisfactory solution to this dilemma, but our approach is to present a propositional framework which, in conjunction with the analytical framework, can then be used in specific cases involving a firm in a particular host state. What follows then, hopefully, will enable one to examine the nature and possible success of multinational enterprise attempts to influence the host-country environment.

This propositional framework is composed of a few critical variables which seem to be important for corporate influence-efforts, but little or no research has been conducted which would confirm or deny the

Table 7-1. Variables Affecting Success or Failure of MNE Influence Attempts: A Propositional Framework

Variables	*More likely to have positive effect*	*More likely to have negative effect*	*Complications*
General Environmental Set			
1. Orientation of host state to direct foreign investment	favorable	unfavorable	
2. Orientation of host state to capitalism	favorable	unfavorable	
3. Degree of political stability and support	stable	unstable (may be able to gain greater political support)	But an unstable government may feel that it is necessary to use resources of MNE and parent gov't. to retain power.
4. Degree of importance of direct foreign investment in general	important	unimportant	But a high degree of importance may lead to greater clamor for exercising independence.
5. Degree of importance of specific MNE	important	unimportant	Also, unimportant MNE may be far enough removed from political notice to enable government to grant requests.
6. General state of relations between host government and parent government	friendly	unfriendly	
Situational Set			
7. Perceived legitimacy of specific MNE	high legitimacy	low legitimacy	
8. Perceived legitimacy of objectives sought	high legitimacy	low legitimacy	
9. Perceived legitimacy of influence tactics used	high legitimacy	low legitimacy	

Table 7-1 Continued

Variables	*More likely to have positive effect*	*More likely to have negative effect*	*Complications*
10. Compatibility of corporate values with target values	high	low	
11. Local or foreign nature of corporate objectives			
a. origin	local	foreign	
b. benefit	local	foreign	
c. style	local	foreign	
12. Local or foreign nature of corporate influence actions			
a. origin	local	foreign	
b. benefit	local	foreign	
c. style	local	foreign	
13. Position of MNE in influencing groups	one of many other actors; single actor if legitimate objective	single actor of debatable legitimacy	Many complications.
14. Pattern of support for MNE objective			
a. Scope	broad	narrow	
b. Intensity	committed	unenthusiastic	
c. Importance of supporters	well-placed	unimportant	
15. Pattern of opposition for MNE objective			
a. Scope	narrow	broad	
b. Intensity	unenthu-siastic	committed	
c. Importance of opponents	unimportant	well-placed	
16. Pattern of indifference for MNE objective			
a. Scope	broad	narrow	Depends on mix support and opposition.
b. Importance of neutrals	unimportant	well-placed	
17. Perceived cost to host state of being influenced			
a. Economic	low	high	generally, low-cost or high-benefit is likely to be more difficult to show than high-cost, low benefit.
b. Political	low	high	
c. Ideological	low	high	
d. Self-image	low	high	

Table 7-1 Continued

Variables	*More likely to have positive effect*	*More likely to have negative effect*	*Complications*
18. Perceived benefit to host state of being influenced			
a. Economic	high	low	
b. Political	high	low	
c. Ideological	high	low	
d. Self-image	high	low	

relationships implicitly hypothesized. Indeed, it should be made clear that very little research of any type has been undertaken about the subject of corporate interaction with host-state political systems, or corporate efforts to influence host states. Tentative propositions about the effect of these variables, regarding the success or failure of multinational enterprise influence-attempts are summarized in Table 7-1.

One set of variables, with the potential to affect the success or failure of influence attempts, is the general environment within which the influence efforts will be undertaken. Some of the more important variables comprising this set are the general orientation of the host state to foreign enterprises, to capitalism, and to the degree of political stability and support for the regime based on the nature of internal political forces. Another variable involves the degree of importance to the host country of foreign investment, in general, and the specific foreign enterprise, in particular, in terms of economic contribution, location, crucial industries, impact on balance of payments accounts, employment, and other similar factors. An additional important component of the environmental set of variables concerns the general state of relations between host country and parent country. It seems likely that great hostility between the two governments will seriously hinder corporate efforts to influence the host-state government, the political process, the political participants, or, perhaps, even the communication system. As an example, newspaper reports indicated that during the India-Pakistan war Americans doing business in India found the environment to be quite hostile, but it would be interesting to examine this case more closely to see whether, indeed, there was such a negative effect. It may not necessarily follow that the more friendly the relations between host and parent governments, the greater the chance for successful influence-attempts. Instead, it is quite possible that there are various threshold levels at work, particularly at the negative end of the continum. Certainly, creative and rigorous comparative research efforts should be undertaken to examine the impact of these environmental variables on corporate influence-attempts.

There are a number of other variables more specific to a particular influence-attempt which are also important determinants of the success or failure of such efforts. This set of variables, involving the receptivity of host-state targets to influence attempts, seems to be quite critical. As discussed earlier, influence is a behavioral relationship, and, as such, it is necessary to assess various characteristics of host-state targets which make them more or less susceptible to efforts to change behavior. One factor of importance is the perceived *legitimacy of the multinational enterprise itself* by the target in the host state, and a reasonable hypothesis would be that the more legitimate the corporation was thought to be, the greater the likelihood of a successful influence-attempt. Perceived legitimacy of the *objective sought* by the multinational firm, and the perceived legitimacy of the specific *influence tactics* used, also seem to be critical elements in determining the effectiveness of efforts to modify the behavior of various targets. An extension of these variables involves the perceived *compatibility of corporate values with target values,* as indicated by the influence actions and goals of the corporation. In spite of the lack of any but the most anecdotal evidence, these variables do seem to be potentially important for the eventual success or failure of the influence attempt.

Contributing to the degree of receptivity of host-state targets to multinational enterprise are target perceptions of *the local or foreign nature of the origin, benefit, and style of corporate objectives and actions.* An objective or action which is thought to have been conceived and developed in the foreign headquarters of an international firm, which is considered to benefit primarily these foreign institutions, and which reflects a "foreign" style or nature, has a greater possibility of being met with resistance by the host-state target than if the opposite characteristics existed. In other words, the conditions specified would make a successful influence-attempt more difficult to achieve.

Another characteristic of the influence attempt, which assumes importance as it is perceived by the target, is the role of the multinational enterprise in the effort. If the foreign corporation is viewed as merely one enterprise joining many others, both domestic and foreign, the possibility of modifying behavior may be greater than if the firm assumes a position of leadership in a narrowly structured group, or if it is the only interested party. But, of course, this tendency may be reversed by the effect of other variables which have been identified.

Contributing to an enterprise's ability to influence the host state is the degree and nature of domestic host-country supporters of the objectives and actions of the firm. Widespread, committed, and well-placed support for the influence objective may facilitate the achievement of desirable modifications of behavior. However, widespread and intense opposition may doom such efforts to failure. A pervasive indifference to the issue at hand, where neither supporters nor opponents are in evidence, may also result in success. These variables, of course, emphasize once again the relational aspect of influence and, therefore, the necessity of examining factors internal to the host state in order to assess the potential for success or failure of corporate influence-attempts. The degree of support, opposition, or indifference, the intensity and breadth of these feelings, and the importance of supporters and opponents in the domestic political and governmental system, may have much to say about the outcome of multinational enterprise influence-attempts.

Two other variables of some import involve the perceived cost or benefit to the host state of being influenced by the multinational enterprise. This cost or benefit can be further divided into cost or benefit of an economic, political ideological, or self-image nature. The implications of perceived cost or benefit on the success of influence attempts are obvious, but it is probably accurate to suggest that, in a majority of states, targets of influence activity will be more predisposed to seeing high costs and low benefits than the reverse. This, of course, adds to the difficulty of successfully modifying host-state behavior. Indeed, it is precisely this factor that multinational enterprises, seeking to institute complementation agreements with several states, as Jack Behrman has suggested, will have to overcome.

The above sets of variables seem to be *some* of the important factors affecting the efforts of international firms to influence host states. It is clear, though, that the tentative propositional framework is overly-simplistic, in that the variables are presented in a discrete fashion, whereas, in fact, they are very much interdependent. Unfortunately, though, very little research has been undertaken regarding the impact of these variables, either singly or in concert with others. In order to go beyond the tentative conjecture suggested here, it is imperative that well-designed and well-executed research projects be implemented to explore the impact of the variables and relationships discussed.

CONCLUSION AND RESEARCH SUGGESTIONS

The frameworks presented should be useful in developing the kind of understanding of foreign political systems which allows for prediction of the demands and action of host societies, with regard to matters of concern to the multinational enterprise. Hopefully, this greater understanding of the host-state environment will result in more sensitive and sensible policies on the part of multinational enterprises. A positive strategy designed to encourage and support various needs and demands of host states, which are compatible with the requirements of international firms may be more possible when the dynamics of the host state are understood. Thus, these frameworks should serve the mutual interests of the host state, the multinational enterprise, and the relationship between them.

Undoubtedly, though, some business executives, academics, policy makers, and ideologues may express concern over the thrust of this chapter, which may be interpreted by some as promoting multinational enterprise meddling in the internal affairs of soverign states. The basic concept of attempts by international firms to influence host states may be objectionable to some. However, to be realistic, it is clear that any relationship involves mutual influence-attempts. No two parties can be involved with one another without the existence of influence, or modifications of behavior. If behavioral changes do not occur, then there is, in essence, no relationship. Realistically, this is the case with multinational enterprises and host states. They are bound to influence one another; they should influence one another in order to establish and maintain a mutually beneficial relationship. Of course, if one believes that there is no place for direct foreign investment, then the entire premise of this chapter is unacceptable. However, it is worth citing again that the host-state international firm relationship implies mutual influence attempts. The objective of this chapter, though, is to present a methodology by which officials of multinational enterprises may analyze different and foreign societies to better understand the nature of the internal political/governmental systems. Hopefully, by increasing analytical ability and substantive knowledge in this area, the incidence of misguided, insensitive, and generally damaging policies and actions of multinational enterprises will be reduced.

As mentioned several times in the body of this chapter, systematic research on the influence relationship between multinational enterprises and host states is virtually nonexistent. Consequently, it is quite easy to indicate broad areas for future research efforts, although the implementation of these suggestions is far more difficult. Beginning with the propositional framework presented in this chapter, there is needed a type of brainstorming effort to identify other variables that may affect the success or failure of corporate influence-attempts. Then, carefully constructed research designs need to be developed which will actually test the importance and effect of each variable, and clusters of variables, upon the ability of multinational enterprises to modify the environment of host countries. While tools like discriminant analysis and factor analysis might be useful, it is more likely that the more simple analytical tools will be appropriate, initially.

Important subsets of this research involve the examination of various corporate characteristics and corporate strategies regarding the influence relationship. Variables such as the nature of the corporation's business activity, the organizational and attitudinal traits, the parent company's nationality, the nationality of subsidiary management, and others may be important. Likewise, an assessment of particular influence-strategies and tactics is in order.

A corollary to this research thrust involves the other part of the relationship, the host state. Research needs to be conducted on the importance of the host-state form of government, politics, economic system, and level of development. Is it more or less difficult to maintain good relations with a regime which is weak and, generally, lacking in widespread domestic support? Might cultural or racial similarity play a role or are recent patterns of hostility-friendship and amount and nature of direct foreign investment incursion more important? One potentially instructive way to pursue research in this area is to identify a multinational corporation-host state relationship which seems to have prospered, in spite of many indicators to the contrary. An in-depth analysis might lead to the discovery of very important characteristics, or behavior patterns, which fostered stable and good relations.

A different thrust of research focuses more on the observable practices and organizations of corporations and host states. Instead of studying the relationship as a form of social interaction, the researcher would be investigating instances of how practitioners behave and interact.

Certainly, both types of research are needed. It is important to find out what is being done currently, but it is also necessary to investigate the impact of various variables on the host state-multinational corporation relationship. Both lines of research should begin to have immediate payoff by uncovering the knowledge which will enable corporate executives and country officials to better manage their respective roles in the multinational enterprise-host state relationship.

Chapter Eight

The Negotiation Era and the Multinational Enterprise

Ashok Kapoor

The multinational enterprise (MNE) and host governments (HGs) in developing countries have interacted with each other within a rapidly changing context in the postwar period. The interaction has been characterized by euphoria, frustration, idealism, and realism. However, one essential feature is that during the past quarter of a century both the MNE and the HG have gained far greater experience in interacting with each other; and, consequently, they have become more realistic of what either group can expect from or contribute to the other.[1] In the 1970s, the relationship between the MNE and HGs in developing countries will be characterized by a growing realism requiring changes of both subtle and pronounced nature on both sides. A central feature of the mood of realism will be the preference of both sides for negotiation as versus confrontation.[2] This paper deals with the subject of negotiation, as observed by the author in the developing countries of Asia. However, the observations have relevance for other developing regions as well.

The key themes of this chapter follow:

1. Both the MNE and HGs in developing countries are recognizing the importance of negotiation versus confrontation as a means of reducing conflicts;
2. An escalation in the areas of conflict between the MNE and HG in developing countries will place even greater weight on negotiation to determine areas of agreement and disagreement;
3. The existing literature and ongoing research in the general subject of international business-government negotiations in developing countries is distressingly limited. It is imperative that a significant research thrust be made in this area;
4. New pedagogical tools must be developed in order to provide orientation to students, executives, and government officials on the nature and process of international business-government negotiation. Additionally, a more

systematic effort should be made to develop simulations which will permit hypotheses generation and hypotheses testing.

NATURE OF NEGOTIATION

The term "negotiation" can be described as follows:

> "... two elements must normally be present for negotiation to take place; there must be both common interests and issues of conflict. Without common interest there is nothing to negotiate for, and without conflict there is nothing to negotiate about.[3]

The negotiation process includes strategies and tactics expressed within a broader framework of interactions between groups with both common and conflicting interests. Each group has its own concept of what is "right," "reasonable," or "appropriate" in negotiations; also, each group has its own expectations of the likely response of an opposing group to an issue, event, or mood. In highlighting the key characteristics of "strategy," Schelling states:

> ... it focuses on the fact that each participant's 'best' choice of action depends on what he expects the other to do, and that 'strategic behavior' is concerned with influencing another's choice by working on his expectation of how one's own behavior is related to his.[4]

Schelling calls this "the theory of interdependent decision."[5]—a fundamental feature of the negotiation process.

The outcome of negotiations is more than just an explicit agreement.

> Negotiation may change the position of the parties and their mutual relations in many ... ways. The outcome may include, for example, tacit understanding between the parties, a clarification of the points of disagreement, a reorientation of national objectives, new commitments to third parties (allies, domestic groups, or world opinion), and propaganda effects. Many of these results may outweigh in importance whatever explicit agreement is arrived at.[6]

International business negotiations take place within a broader framework than domestic negotiations.

> The art of politics and the concepts of social science can become as important, or even more important, to the success of an investment negotiation as hard-headed technical and financial calculations or a carefully prepared legal and administrative basis for an overseas organization.[7]

THE NEGOTIATION ERA IN INTERNATIONAL BUSINESS-GOVERNMENT RELATIONS

Several interrelated reasons account for the emergence of a mood on the part of the MNE and HG in developing countries favoring negotiation versus confrontation.

CHANGES IN INTERNATIONAL RELATIONS

The 1970s are demonstrating the important influence on the global community of the new multinational powers—the European Economic Community and Japan—in addition to the traditional bipolar power structure limited to the United States and Russia. The new multinational powers are developing their own spheres of influence. And the economic strength of a multinational power will strongly influence its negotation position and process. To the degree that the MNE is an essential component of such economic power, it will act as both a facilitating and a hindering force in the negotiations between the multinational powers.

The new multinational enterprises from Western Europe, particularly those from Japan, and a handful which are indigenous to developing countries have a far greater tradition of collaborative and consultative relationships with their respective home governments than is true for the American multinational enterprise (AMNE). Yet another group of MNEs is in Communist countries where the distinction between the enterprise and the home government is limited, if it exists at all.[8]

The essential point is that negotiations between the multinational powers will definitely include recognition and concern for their own MNEs. One consequence is likely to be the need for the AMNE to seek a closer affiliation with relevant governments, particularly the U. S. government, in order to promote and protect its interests in the larger negotiation process between the multinational powers.

Several critical questions require research. In what ways will the realignment process between the multinational powers effect the negotiation position and process of the MNE in dealing with the home and host-country governments? In what ways will the relationship between the new MNEs, with their respective home governments affect the relationship between the AMNE and the U. S. government? Will the developing countries view the MNEs as direct tools of the multinational powers, and, if so, what are the implications for negotiation strategies of the MNE and HGs in developing countries?

GROWING INTERNATIONAL COMPETITION

The AMNE will face intense competition from the new MNEs. For example, Japanese foreign direct investors accept terms and conditions of investment which are significantly different from those normally sought by American investors. Furthermore, the objectives and terms of transfer of resources by enterprises in Communist countries are different from those of enterprises within capitalist systems.

The growing competition has created a larger range of alternative sources of supply for developing countries, resulting in improving their negotiation position vis-a-vis the AMNE. To the extent that the AMNE has been the dominant investor, the new competition will result in greater need for interacton and negotiation between the AMNE and host governments.[9]

The negotiations faced by the AMNE are likely to be more difficult and demanding than those faced by the new MNEs. The large investment position of the AMNE, on a multinational basis, exposes it to attacks and criticism by various groups. The sheer size of the AMNE will impose special demands from a negotiation standpoint which are not likely to apply to the lesser MNEs. Also, the AMNE will have to be far more cautious in negotiating in order not to establish undesirable precedents affecting operations on a multinational basis. While host governments will attempt to promote national interests in negotiations, the AMNE will have to protect its multinational interests. The same characteristic will apply to the new MNEs, but, for the time being at least, their scope and range of activities are quite limited as compared to the AMNE.

The growing international competition with a larger and more diversified cast of characters suggests several areas of research. In what ways have the new MNEs influenced the negotiation position of the AMNE? What changes are required in the MNE and HG-approach to negotiation, as their respective perception of power changes? More specifically, in what ways is the approach and process of negotiation of the MNE influenced as its perception of power vis-à-vis the HG shifts from "more powerful" to "equal in power" to "less powerful"? And, conversely, what is the effect on the HGs approach to negotiation as it considers itself to be more powerful vis-à-vis the MNE?

REVOLUTION IN INTERNATIONAL COMMUNICATION

By and large, the physical methods exist for almost instantaneous global dissemination of information. Even more important is that HGs place increasing emphasis upon the use of information acquired on a worldwide basis in negotiating with the MNE and with internal interest groups. The MNE has always possessed a major comparative advantage in this area. In the future, however, the MNE will retain an important advantage, but the extent of the gap between the MNE and HGs will be reduced with significant implications for international business-government negotiation.

One critical implication is that decisions in one part of the world will be reviewed and assessed for their relevance in other parts of the world.[10] This will necessitate far greater emphasis on precedent orientation by the AMNE in particular.

The international communications revolution is a relatively recent phenomenon, but it poses several important questions for research. In what specific ways does it influence the negotiation process from the viewpoint of the MNE and HG? Are HGs likely to utilize a "pooled" approach to information, and, if so, with what effect? Will such efforts at pooling of information encourage collaboration in other areas by HGs?

THE NEW ELITES

Both the MNE and HGs possess a growing body of officials/managers with a less provincial outlook and a relatively greater understanding of development requirements of both nations and enterprises. This greater degree of commonalty between the new elites as opposed to that possessed by their predecessors is likely to encourage better understanding and a stronger tendency for negotiation versus confrontation.

A significant shift in favor of technocrats versus political ideologists is already taking place in some Asian countries. This feature is particularly prevalent in countries where the political leaders are firmly established, and can turn their attention to grappling with the issues of development. Such leaders are offering greater responsibility to technocrats, not only to interpret and implement policies, but also to play a growing role in the formulation of policies.[11] The technocrats are acutely conscious of the wide range of problems faced by their countries and the limited resources available to them. More specifically, on the question of policies toward foreign investments, the technocrats recognize that the tendency toward greater restrictions on foreign investors is not confined to any particular industry, but extends throughout. Therefore, the conflict-issues being faced in a particular industry are likely to occur in other industries. Negotiation, and not confrontation, will add to their learning and is likely to offer means for reducing conflicts.

The new breed of international executive differs from his predecessoı He is, typically, an internationalist in outlook, having to contend with senior management levels which largely still retain a domestic-market (U.S.A.) orientation. As with the technocrats, the new international executives recognize the futility of confrontations.

It is essential to note that a new breed is beginning to be found within both the MNE and HGs in developing countries. And during the 1970s, this characteristic will facilitate a greater dialogue between the two groups.

Several questions for research are presented by this characteristic. What conditions are necessary for the continued effectiveness of the new breed in HGs and in the MNE? What problems characterize the efforts of this new breed in educating their own most senior officials/executives to the realities of international business and governments in developing countries? Given the greater commonalty between negotiators from the two groups, issues of a technical nature pose a lesser problem. Rather, questions of nature, role, and contributions of the MNE to host societies have gained in importance. Not only has the incidence of negotiation increased, but the content of negotiation has changed from the relatively technical to the largely subjective and philosophical. Therefore, what new problems and prospects does this characteristic pose for international business-government negotiations?

RELATIVE INDEPENDENCE OF DECISIONS

HGs in developing countries are now making relatively independent decisions, free from foreign economic or political pressures, short of those normally associated with being a member of the community of nations. The independence of decisions places greater responsibility on the decision makers because an adverse outcome cannot be blamed on a foreign foe. Additionally, growing awareness of the realities of development on the part of opinion-forming elites in developing countries requires a cautious and informed approach on the part of decision makers. Realism, independence, and responsibility favor negotiation versus confrontation as a means of resolving conflicts.

The independence of decisions reached during the 1970s is likely to persist for some time to come. Therefore, one implication for the MNE and HGs is to evaluate with care the modifications they are willing to accept.

DIRECTIONS FOR RESEARCH

Despite the importance of international business-government negotiations in developing countries, the current body of published information is distressingly limited,[12] and so is the amount of research being done in this area at present. Research on nationalism, international business-government relations, and other important areas relates to the general question of negotiation. But research specifically in the issue of negotiation is urgently required. The MNE and HGs in developing countries have entered into an era of negotiation, and a body of literature and pedagogical tools related to the subject will enhance the participants' understanding of the characteristics and issues involved.

The most useful approach, at present, is to develop a series of case studies of different types of international business negotiations. Conceptual frameworks will be possible only after we have engaged in sufficient empirical research to be able to identify the essential characteristics and the probably relationships between them. Also, the negotiation process incorporates a wide range of issues wherein the central figure is the manner in which the variables interact. A case approach permits appropriate recognition and treatment of the necessary features.

The following pages present a brief description of an illustrative list of the types of international-business negotiation situations which should be studied.[13]

1. Transnational ventures between foreign governments and MNE. An example of such a venture is the Madras fertilizer project involving the government of India, National Iranian Oil Company, and Standard Oil of Indiana. This form of transnational venture will grow in importance, especially in capital-intensive and strategic industries. Also, it would show how sovereign states negotiate when entering into a business venture, and the specific and unique characteristics confronted by a MNE in negotiating with two governments would highlight an important form of MNE involvement in developing countries in the coming years.
2. MNE from Communist countries and transfer of resources. The USSR offered to provide assistance for the Bokaro steel plant in India when the U. S. A. declined. U. S. Steel was to have been the primary contractor for the project, if the U. S. government had proceeded with it. This case offers an interesting example of negotiations on a government-to-government basis within the context of the Cold War and the potential role played by the MNE. Russian assistance to developing countries is growing, and the MNE will need to understand the negotiation approach of an increasingly important competitor.
3. Large foreign direct investments in joint ventures. The joint venture between Chrysler and Mitsubishi offers an example. Such cases reveal the ways in which forces of nationalism, national interest, and other aspects of international business express themselves in a specific context. Also, while technically a joint venture between two private companies, large ventures of the Chrysler-Mitsubishi type invariably require close and effective consultation and approval by the host-country government. The negotiation processes revealed by the larger cases are generally applicable to smaller and more typical situations of foreign investment.
4. Large foreign direct investment in a joint venture. A proposed investment by Mitsubishi in Thailand for a petrochemical complex resulted in failure. This type of situation permits learning from failure which is at least as instructive as a successful venture.[14] While the successful Chrysler-Mitsubishi negotiations reveal the approaches and strategies used by Mitsubishi (in Japan) as the local partner, the unsuccessful venture in Thailand would reveal the approaches and strategies adopted by Mitsubishi as the foreign investor. Some degree of comparison between the

two roles permit tentative observations, which might subsequently be extended to other cases. Japanese direct foreign investment faces criticism from several Southeast Asian countries–the strongest from Thailand. A study of the negotiation process in Thailand might shed some light on similar problems encountered in other Asian countries.

5. Foreign disinvestment negotiation process. One instance of such disinvestment is Esso's withdrawal from the fertilizer industry in the Philippines. A growing number of disinvestments are occurring. The relative power of the foreign investor vis-à-vis the HG differs from the time the firm made the initial investment. A company simply cannot dismantle and remove a plant. Conversely, the position of the HG is stronger because a local plant has been established. Therefore, in what ways is the foreign disinvestment negotiation process different from the foreign investment negotiation process?
6. Consortium to consortium negotiation. The Organization of Petroleum Exporting Countries negotiated effectively with the private oil companies, which were organized into a consortium. It is more than likely that companies in other industries might adopt a consortium approach in undertaking foreign direct investments, especially in capital intensive industries. The legal limitations might be removed if modifications in interpretation of U. S. antitrust laws are actually implemented. Developing countries are aware of their weaker negotiation position, and are exploring possibilities of some form of collaboration.

How should research be conducted? It will require the collaboration of professors in the country in which the situations occured. The benefits will be: greater access to information especially because of the sensitive nature of the negotiations and greater know-how within the local context; another step forward toward building research relationships and local expertise; and a greater probability of funding by host-country institutions.

The collaborators, in a formal or informal sense, are the actual participants in the negotiations between the MNE and HG. Many characteristics of the negotiations are dependent upon subjective factors of interactions between two or more individuals. Therefore, a proper understanding of the negotiation process requires a strong and persistent effort to re-create the nature and tone of such personal relations and interactions. Additionally, collaboration of at least one of the primary groups is necessary in order to encourage the opposing group to cooperate in presentation of its side of the story.

Collaboration with scholars in other diciplines such as political science and international relations is also necessary. Scholars in these fields have researched the subject of negotiation to a far greater extent than their colleagues in the field of international business. The theories and conceptual frameworks developed in these disciplines are relevant to the study of international business negotiations. However, the orientation and objectives of the research should be carefully delineated from the very start because scholars in international business have a significantly different orientation from those in political science and international relations.

In addition to the development of a body of case studies, new pedagogical tools must be developed to teach and study the nature and process of international business negotiations. Simulations have been experimented with successfully at the Graduate School of Business Administration of New York University, and have been successfully applied at the Economic Development Institute of the International Bank for Reconstruction and Development. The results include a "players" manual, a videotape with "voice over" analysis, a courtroom-type transcript of negotiations, with appropriate comments and analysis of the negotiation tactics and strategies, and a modificaton of an existing game of international diplomacy for international business-government negotiation purposes.

The current experiment at the New York University is only a preliminary thrust in this general direction. Much more work is needed to develop the field. The effort will be worthwhile because simulations, when properly conducted, permit rapid training of students, executives, and government officials; and they permit the generation and testing of hypotheses. Real life negotiation situations have been simulated in the classroom with startling similarity of processes and strategies.

Chapter Nine

Perspectives for the Future

John Fayerweather,
David H. Blake and
J. Alex Murray

The purpose of this final chapter is to convey the main insights on international business-government affairs developed in the workshop discussion. The chapter is not a simple summary of the discussion because of two characteristics of the workshop.

First, while the sessions followed a broad topical outline, the comments of eighteen participants—with diverse professional and geographic backgrounds—inevitably ranged over a wide territory.* Second, because of time constraints, some ideas were presented very briefly, and connecting links among ideas were often not set forth explicitly.

These characteristics were not a significant deterrent to the on-the-spot stimulation of the thoughts of the participants. But on the printed page a summary of such discussion would be unduly erratic and confusing. The authors have therefore re-sorted the comments of the participants into what they feel is an orderly structure, and added connective tissue where it seemed appropriate in order to present an effective understanding of the ideas under consideration.

The resulting chapter may be characterized as the authors' perception of the aspects of international business-government affairs covered by the workshop, based mainly on the comments of the participants, but with their own viewpoints influencing its organization and interpretation.

THE STRUCTURE OF INTERNATIONAL ECONOMIC DECISION-MAKING

The raison d'etre for the workshop was the easily observed fact that major changes are under way in the international structure of relations among governments and business. The discussions were concerned essentially with exploration of how the structure would evolve, and the requirements for

*See roster of participants in the front of the book.

effective participation by both business and governments in the emerging processes and relationships.

The essence of the evolution of the structure lies in the movement toward a new system for the control of resource allocation and related economic decisions. The principal characteristic of the emerging system is the movement toward a much greater degree of internationalization of economic processes, and as a consequence, a greater degree of internationally centralized control. While this process has sound economic logics, it entails major readjustments and tensions which were a primary aspect of the workshop discussion. The evolving structure, and the problems accompanying it, involve such varied and complicated elements that there is a grave risk of oversimplification in any discussion of them. The comments of each workshop participant inevitably focused on limited facets of this picture. However, after piecing them together, they provide a quite effective set of insights into the key issues.

There was little discussion in the workshop of the logics of the movement toward greater international integration of economies. The participants accepted implicitly the benefits of the substantial degree of interdependence and integration of technology, capital, and production which are a reality in the modern world. Likewise, they did not dwell on the equally obvious basic function of the multinational firm as a principal agent in this internationalization process. The issues which occupied the participants lay rather in the degree to which resource allocation and economic decision-making should progress to an international level, the role of various participants in economic decision making and the interactions which would influence the process by which the evolution took place.

While the trend toward a greater degree of international economic control in which the multinational firm is a major factor was generally accepted, two major deterrents to this evolution were cited. The first point, which was developed most fully by Jack Behrman, is the basic reaction at any level of societal grouping to the shift of control and decision making to the higher levels. He cited as a parallel the conflict between neighborhoods and cities, as the latter attempted to make decisions beneficial to the collective interests of several neighborhoods. The internationalization of economic decision-making inevitably arouses the same sort of localized resistance in both home and host governments and individual groups within nations. The multinational firm is a conspicuous target for resistance of this sort, although the same basic feelings are relevant to internation decision-making by nonbusiness institutions. However, the problem is complicated by the fact that most nations perceive the multinational firm not simply as an international entity, but as a foreign one, which to some extent, represents the interests and power of another nation.

The other basic deterrent is the pattern of limitations of the free-market system, given the major constraints on its functioning which exist in the world today. Mr. Gillespie addressed this issue early in the discussion. He observed that private enterprise, motivated primarily by profit, is an effective instrument for the allocation of capital in society only to a limited degree, given the varied goals of societies. The free-market system, dependent primarily on profit motivation, cannot be expected to achieve decisions satisfying to all social goals, so the role of government is inevitable. In an international context, this problem assumes special characteristics because of the greater prominence of noneconomic goals important to individual nations.

Dr. Robinson cited another dimension of limitation of the free-market system as applied to multinational firms. In many cases, he observed, we are dealing with countries which are too small for effective competitive interaction of firms. The results of this problem are readily observed in two equally questionable outcomes in economic structure: on the one hand, the situations in which one or two multinational firms monopolize a small market and competition is not vigorous enough and, on the other hand, situations wherein a large number of firms establish themselves within a country, all on a scale too small to achieve optimum economies of production.

These considerations did not influence the participants to turn away from the free-market system. Indeed, the consensus was generally favorable toward its maximum utilization. However, there was realistic acceptance that the free-market system had to operate within a greater degree of governmentally-determined constraints in order to be effective for the achievement of social purposes of particular nations within the internationalized economy.

As broad generalizations the participants readily accepted these two deterrents—resistance to centralization and limitations of reliance on the free-market system. The questions which they found difficult to answer, and which remain as areas for future research, concern the degree to which each deterrent will affect the role of the multinational firm as an internationally-integrated economic decision-maker. It was implied by a number of comments that, the centralization of decision making having moved ahead quite strongly during the 1960s, we are currently in a period when resistance to centralization, reinforced by nationalism and questioning of the free-market system, are gaining momentum.

These implications underlay the recurring comments on the evolution of intergovernmental means of accomplishing the internationalization of economic decision-making. This concept, of course, has been the subject of great expectations for many years, and has received a major boost from the accomplishments of the European Economic Community. Elsewhere in the world, however, intergovernmental economic arrangements have made little progress, and, even in Europe, in such vital areas as rationalization of research and production in high technology fields, it has moved very slowly.

The workshop participants were not content to accept this degree of progress as a limitation for the future. They clearly felt that a movement toward greater intergovernmental arrangements was desirable in spite of the resurgence of nationalistic thinking within nations and that the essential requirement was to probe the possibilities in various directions. Olivier Giscard d'Estaing gave importance to this general attitude by pointing out the inability of a purely nation-oriented government to serve the full needs of the people, when an internationalized approach to economic questions will result in more beneficial results for them. Thus, some type of multinational governmental decision-making, he felt, was an essential requirement. Others dealt with the question in terms of more specific possibilities. For example, Jerome Rosow felt that the Organization for Economic Cooperation and Development (OECD) will become a more active medium of influence in bringing governments together. More specifically from his own industry's viewpoint, he anticipated a greater degree of multination government discussion as a response to the joint governmental action of the Organization for Petroleum Exporting Countries (OPEC). Professor Kobayashi signalled an important element of progress in this direction in the position the Japanese government has recently adopted by favoring the development of an international code for multinational firms. Professor Fayerweather suggested that paralleling the mutations of multinational firms (to be mentioned later), one might anticipate the development of a variety of mutations of intermediaries to facilitate international economic agreements between governments. While OECD is conspicuous now as a good candidate for success, he proposed that other types of groupings for different functions were likely to appear as time went on. Dr. Behrman's comments on international rationalization of production, elaborated upon in his chapter, figured prominently in this line of discussion.

The workshop discussion was notably lacking in insights as to variables which might determine the pace at which development of inter-government economic decision-making might proceed. This gap suggests a substantial area for future research. Jack Behrman has completed an intensive study in Latin America, indicating the major deterrents to production rationalization there, despite obvious advantages in production costs and capital utilization, together with benefits from equitable employment distribution. It would appear that significant changes in attitudes in the trade-off between economic benefits and other social goals, as well as critical factors in the political decision-making process, are preconditions for progress. We have little information now upon which to judge the prospects of movement in this direction, or ways in which it may be facilitated. Dr. Behrman did make one suggestion in the workshop which is significant in this respect, however. He proposed that multinational firms might have an important role as negotiating intermediaries, or, at least, initiators to bring countries together in making production agreements. There are already a handful of cases in which a company has persuaded two Latin American countries to allow it to manufacture one product in each, with a free flow of goods into the other.

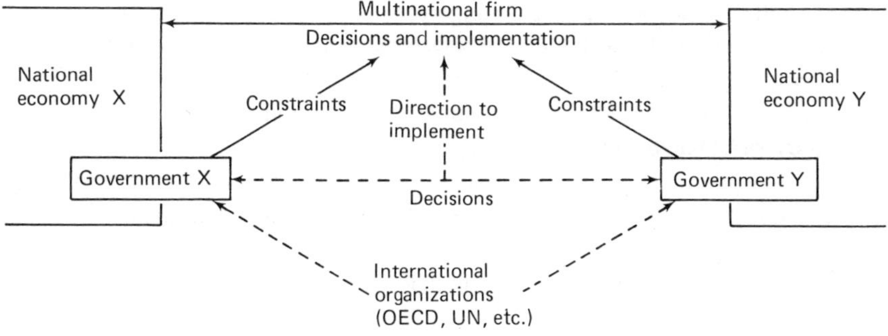

Figure 9-1. International Economic Resource Allocation System

While there may be a limited number of possibilities for this sort of process, he felt that they would represent a useful start in the evolution of intergovernmental production arrangements.

The main thrust of these elements of the discussion can be summarized by reference to Figure 9-1. There is a movement toward the internationalization of economic organization and decision making. Two main instrumentalities for accomplishing this exist: first, the multinational firm, guided by a combination of governmental direction and the profit motive; second, intergovernmental arrangements, either worked out directly or through intermediary organizations (UN, OECD, etc.). To date, the greater portion of the internationalization has been accomplished by means of the first alternative, but the movement in that direction is increasingly constrained by resistances at the national level to centralization, and dissatisfaction with the limited degree to which social goals are satisfied by the free-market system. The immediate result is an increasing load of constraints upon the role of the multinational firm, imposed on a country-by-country basis. This process tends to disrupt the capabilities of the multinational firm to achieve the international economic integration function, but does not substantially alter the primacy of its role as the dominant world institution performing this function.

As indicated by the dotted lines in Figure 9-1, the potentials for intergovernment agreement to take over a greater portion of the international economic decision-making still are very largely undeveloped. In view of the strengths of the motivation leading to the conditions and restrictions placed upon the performance of the multinational firm, one would expect the intergovernmental process increasingly to be employed to achieve the benefits of international economic integration in a manner more satisfactory for social criteria. As that occurs, the multinational firm would become, increasingly, the agent for the governments in the accomplishment of agreements, rather than the independent decision-making organization developing integrative

systems itself. The workshop discussions were useful in opening up critical questions along these lines, but clearly much needs to be learned before the future evolution will be clear.

GOALS OF NATIONS AND FIRMS

In the evolution of the international economic decision-making structure, the goals of nations and firms occupy a prominent place. A considerable part of the discussion by the workshop participants was devoted to this subject.

HOST-GOVERNMENT OBJECTIVES

Discussions of the objectives of host governments tend to concentrate on a variety of subjects which bear on the economic well-being of the nation. While these elements were present throughout the workshop discussion, it is significant that, at the very start, a higher level of objectives was emphasized, and that this level was frequently referred to as the discussion proceeded. This recurring theme was that the basic goal of nations was the enhancement of the dignity of man. Businessmen and even host-government officials may often lose sight of this fact in their preoccupation with economic affairs. However, its dominance as an overriding criterion will ever assert itself through political processes, and its influence can clearly be discerned in the character of the positions taken by governments around the world.

The objective is to obtain both greater benefits for the citizens of a nation and most significant, a greater sense of participation in the decisions and processes by which those benefits are managed and produced. As one workshop participant observed, it is quite possible that host governments are often misguided or unrealistic in their expectations of the enhancement of the dignity of their citizens which will result from particular demands placed upon multinational firms. The Chilean case was cited as a demonstration of how the emotional thrust of national desires might have adverse total impact upon national welfare. But this shortcoming in no way diminishes the basic importance of humanistic goals for the governments.

A second overall theme which pervaded the discussion was the diversity in concepts of goals and priorities within host nations. Failure to recognize this diversity was identified as a significant source of difficulty in the interaction of governments and multinational firms. For example, Mr. Rosow commented that it is quite natural for some nations to trade off some degree of economic growth for social goals. Dr. Laserna observed that a major problem lay in the general practice of applying concepts of economic development growing out of experience in the advanced countries to the situation of less developed countries to which they may be quite inappropriate. The value standards and social structure in Latin American countries may call

for a different approach from that which North American and European firms may advocate on the basis of their experience. Mr. Boothalingham expressed the Indian philosophy of socialism, as distinguished from individualism, which leads his countrymen to give higher priority to better distribution of benefits at the expense of some loss of economic efficiency, if such choice be required. The latter two participants noted that value standards, such as the Protestant ethic, which multinational firms carried with them often were an impediment to integration because of values emphasizing less intense work achievement, and other goals in host societies. These points of view are stated briefly and scarcely comprehensive descriptions of the range of objectives for host governments. They are sufficient, however, to illustrate the diversity.

In addition to the variety of social and economic goals which characterize nations, Professor Crozier stressed the diversity of goals within a nation which creates a significant problem when defining national goals. He pointed out that it is difficult for the members of a nation to communicate effectively with one another and to agree on such a basic question as the type of growth they seek. While there may be considerable range of widely-shared goals and values, the individuals and groups within a society will have a number of differences in objectives. What appear as the national goals of a country at any one time are, therefore, inevitably a compromise of priorities within the expressed goals of the components of the nation. They will be the result of varying attitudes, pressures, and capabilities.

This aspect of the situation is significant in at least two respects. First, national goals of this nature are inevitably subject to change. As attitudes shift among the components of the society, or the strength of various components changes, the goals expressed by the government will change. Professor Litvak identified, as one major aspect of this instability, the evolution of national industrial strategies. Canada, for example, is currently shifting from a traditional strategy, based on natural resources and protected manufacturing, to greater emphasis on internationally competitive manufacturing. Second, the compromise and shifting character of the goals means that the strategy of a nation and its government is often ill-defined and, therefore, hard for the multinational firm to discern. Both business and government participants in the workshop commented on this as a major complicating factor in the efforts of firms to relate themselves to goals of host nations. Some, like Olivier Giscard d'Estaing, felt that the governments had an obligation to define their strategies more clearly, as a responsibility to their own people as well as an aid to external groups, such as the firms who performed a role within their societies. Others, however, agreed with Ashok Kapoor's view that clear, long-term strategies were a luxury beyond the reach of most governments. These limitations cast real doubt on the ability of host-national governments to perform the roles in international economic decision-making, considered above, as effectively as might be postulated theoretically. It is uncertain, therefore, whether they will develop in the role as fully as might be anticipated, or whether, having achieved certain roles by virtue of their power, they will function with the effectiveness which their citizens expect. Some participants felt that there might be opportunities for multinational firms to utilize their technical expertise to aid governments in the definition of goals and the evaluation of various means of achieving them. This function, of course, would have to be undertaken in a sensitive and apolitical fashion.

So far as the functioning of the system is concerned, the limitations of the host government create operating problems for multinational firms, which were commented upon in several ways by the participants. The system assumes that in its economic decision-making, the multinational firms will adjust to the host-national goals. Several participants noted, however, that it is difficult to do this when the goals are poorly defined or not readily ascertained. It was proposed that the firms could do a more effective job in environmental analysis, which would provide some clarification of national interests, to supplement the views expressed by the government. But even this avenue has limitations, so the discussion clearly indicated that the determination and communication of host-national goals was an area requiring further attention.

Within the broad context established by these points, the participants generally concurred that the goal of economic progress was primary. Its primacy is based not only on the general desire to provide economic betterment for citizens of a nation, but also upon recognition, as Mr. Boothalingham expressed it, of the fact that economic means are necessary to accomplish some of the most important social and cultural advances which are so earnestly sought. Thus, amidst the confusion of assorted and changing priorities among political, economic, social, and cultural goals, there is assurance that a major thrust toward economic progress will persist, which provides the basic raison d'etre for the role of the multinational firm in foreign societies.

In one sense, these elements add up to a picture of confused and uncertain goals among host governments. In another sense, however, they provide quite a clear picture of the future context to which multinational firms must relate. The prime role of economic development establishes a strong basis for continued participation of multinational firms in host societies because of their capabilities, notably the capital and skills they can command. On the other hand, the growing sensitivity of host nations to the dignity-of-man aspect, the variety of concepts of the meaning of that aspect in different societies, and the assorted and changing character of the internal determinants of national goals assure that multinational firms must interact and be responsive to many different contexts for years to come.

OBJECTIVES OF MULTINATIONAL FIRMS

Against this picture of diversity among host governments, the participants were able to treat the multinational firm as a much more consistent institution. Indeed, Mario Laserna pointed out, as a striking feature of our times, that for the first time in history the whole world was working toward the evolution of a common institution in the multinational firm. Up to this point, global society in all respects—religion, law, and so forth—has been characterized by diversity. But now, at least in the free world, we are finding that a common institution is providing effective social performance. He concluded from this that the multinational firm had substantial capability in its basic character to contribute to common problems experienced around the world, even though those problems exist in societies which are diverse in many characteristics.

The workshop discussion tended to concentrate on conventional concepts of the firm, as motivated primarily by economic goals. This point of view is probably natural, in light of the dominant role of the government and business participants in the discussion. Host-government officials deal mostly with firms within economic negotiations and, therefore, conceive the firm to be primarily oriented in this plane. The businessmen are preoccupied from day to day with the sales-cost-profit calculus, which again emphasizes the economic goals of the firm.

However, two other concepts of the objectives of the firm appeared from time to time in the discussion, and seem equally important in considering relations with governments. The first is that, in the broadest view, the primary goal of the firm is to survive, and, closely related to that, the desire to grow. The economic elements are so closely intertwined with these goals of survival and growth that the two may be indistinguishable at times. However, it is important to recognize the primacy of the survival and growth elements, because in many situations they will lead to different responses from simple economic performance in international operations. The difference is often evident in the willingness of companies to maintain activities at minimal profit, or even loss, in order to hold a market position or sustain an organization. Often this sort of decision may be identified simply as the difference between short-term and long-term economic goals. But, the workshop participants accepted the survival-growth objectives as primary in the thinking of managements.

The second concept is that of the firm as an institution providing social, cultural, and political satisfaction, as well as economic performance. To some degree, these goals are performed within the confines of the firm—notably in the major role which work activity serves in the social lives of employees. To some degree, they require a high degree of interaction with the surrounding society. Professor Robinson put his finger on a significant element of this dual role when he observed that firms often seem to be maximizing their political goals, while just satisfying economic goals. For many top business executives, the power which they exercise, both internally and externally,is as important a reward as income, and these personal goals are satisfied through the political power of the firms which they direct. In any discussion of international business-government relations, therefore, the political role of the firm must be given important recognition.

The social and cultural elements may not be so conspicuous at the government level, but they are important indirectly because of the impact they have upon the host society. Michel Crozier pointed out the potentials of this characteristic in host societies. The firm may contribute in two respects beyond its economic role. First, it may give prestige to new ways of doing things as a cultural-change agent. Second, it may facilitate new alignments of groups in society. Both roles provide new opportunities for individual identity.

The significance of looking beyond the obvious economic goals of the firm lies in the response of managements to the variety of situations which the differences of host-national goals have created. The essence of this response would appear to be a high degree of adaptability. While business firms have often been characterized as rather rigid in their outlook, the workshop discussion emphasized that the survival-growth objective resulted in a high degree of fundamental flexibility, and, indeed, the business firm would not appear to differ appreciably from other major social institutions in this respect. A substantial degree of inflexibility is a natural concomitant of ongoing strength and stability. But the capacity to adapt to basic environmental conditions is feasible. The historic evolution of the Catholic church and British parliamentry government come readily to mind as excellent examples. Likewise, the concept of an institution which serves as a vehicle for the achievement of social, cultural, and political goals of participants suggests that the institution may naturally adapt and evolve when the nature of the individual goals differs from place to place and time to time.

In essence, therefore, the multinational firm must have a capacity for economic performance in order to survive and to serve the interests of those participating in it and served by it. But there may be a high degree of flexibility in the adjustments it will make to survive and perform these roles in the varied circumstances which the host-government goals present to it.

The other set of goals of the multinational firm which are significant here are those which pertain to its global orientation. The workshop participants concurred in the view that virtually all multinational firms are now, and will be for many years to come, essentially national companies with extensive international operations. That is, they are based in a particular country, and recognize the primary sovereignty of the government of that country wherever there may be a conflict of sovereignties with foreign governments. The majority of their stockholders are usually in the same country. Thus, the management, to a high degree, has a home-country national orientation. Nonetheless, a number of managements of larger multinational firms are already showing a substantial degree of nonnational or transnational outlook and a trend toward further evolution in this direction is to be expected. In a variety of situations, a company will make decisions with a global goal in mind, rather than serving the interests of any one country, including its home society.

The global strategy goals of the multinational firm affect host-nation relations because they diminish the degree to which the firm is willing to adapt to strictly national objectives. The noteworthy problems lie in the areas of production and export allocation, companies seeking a rational global logistic scheme whereas each country would like to have a factory within its own borders, exporting to as many countries as possible. But, great problems also lie in the present and potential relation to home-country goals, so it is best to move to them, and to elaborate upon their implications.

HOME-GOVERNMENT OBJECTIVES

The problems with the home government are complicated by its dual role with relation to the multinational firm, on the one hand as a supporter, and on the other hand as an antagonist. Since multinational firms are still essentially national firms with foreign operations, the major role of the home government is as a supporter or ally. However, as the transnational characteristics increase, the home government finds itself cast more and more into conflict in its relations with the firm.

In considering the first role, a little conceptualization is useful. The multinational firm may be considered as essentially an agent of the home country in the exercise of international economic activities. While, in an immediate sense, it is deploying company resources abroad and maximizing profit on them for the benefit of stockholders, in a broader sense it is doing the same thing for national resources for the benefit of the nation as a whole. Thus, to a substantial degree, its goals and those of the home nation are the same. Under the theories of free-market economy, it is presumed that it will serve both host- and home-nation goals adequately, in the pursuit of its own interest without the intervention of the government. In practice, as already noted, host governments do not accept this theoretical assumption, and to varying degrees they act to promote their national interests by means which override free economic processes.

This circumstance creates one of the strong influences affecting the role of the home government. When the host government intervenes to affect the interest of the multinational firm, the national interests of the home nation are immediately involved, and the question arises as to whether the home government should intervene on behalf of the firm. In major expropriation cases, when it can help to protect the assets of the firm, the arguments for intervention are very strong. In a great many less prominent situations, however, it is quite uncertain whether or not the home government should intervene and, if so, in what ways.

A second influence is the varying character of government-business relations in different home nations. In the United States, there is a tradition of minimal government intervention, and this, by and large, has governed the role of the U. S. government in the very limited support provided for the activities of multinational firms. However, a greater degree of involvement is found in Europe and, even more, in Japan where the government has traditionally played a major role in industrial strategy. As the multinational firms of other countries become more active, and competition for opportunities abroad becomes greater, the question of the degree of involvement of home governments is therefore subject to competitive pressures.

Turning to the other side of the coin, we must consider the role of the home government when the global strategy goals of the firm are in conflict with the national interest of the home country. This issue first became prominent in the United States in the 1960s, when the capital allocation strategy of multinational firms conflicted with the government concept of national interest in the balance of payments. It should be noted that the firms believed that the national interest was, in fact, better served by their concept of investment than by the constraints exerted by the government. Nonetheless, the potentials for conflict were amply illustrated. Currently, the same type of issue is posed in the debate on production-allocation strategy centered on the Burke-Hartke bill, some elements of the national government feeling that national interest in employment of labor is not served by the decisions of the companies. Again, it is debatable as to who is right and where the true national interest lies.

As we have already observed, such debates have also characterized many of the issues between host governments and multinational firms. There is a substantial problem within countries in the diversity of views and interests which must be blended by the government in order to arrive at a proper determination of national goals. It serves no practical purpose here to argue that a particular determination by a government is unsound as an assessment of true national interest. So far as international business-government affairs are concerned, what we must deal with is the reality of national goals as conceived by the prevailing government. If on investment policy and now on employment policy, the U. S. government determines a particular position which is in conflict with the international goals of the firms, then that is the reality of the interaction between the two which must be dealt with.

The implications of these aspects of the dual role of the home government, in pursuit of national goals, was well illustrated in the discussion of the workshop participants of the ideas about international integration of production, advanced in Jack Behrman's chapter. His concept proposes arrangements by which there is some blending of the global production-allocation goals of the firm, and the interest of host nations in a satisfactory combination of participation in production and adequate economic benefits. But, as the discussion in the workshop developed, this sort of arrangement may raise issues of home-country national interest which will require a role for the home government.

On the support side, there is a question of how far U. S. companies, for example, may go in working out multigovernment arrangements for the allocation of production activities abroad without the involvement of the U.S. government. To some degree, this has been done already in Latin America, where U. S. firms like IBM have entered into complementation agreements involving two or more countries. Ford is working out an arrangement in Southeast Southeast Asia involving a group of countries among which production will be shared for manufacture of a vehicle to be sold in the region. Still, these are limited efforts at an early stage and it seems likely that, if such arrangements were to multiply and if as complications arose between different governments in the later stages of their operation, the U. S. government will find itself in a supporting role, just as it has in the more complex problems of investment in the extractive industries.

On the other hand, these arrangements have potential implications for home-country goals which may be at odds with corporate global aims, thus involving the antagonist role. The critical interest of all home governments in national employment is readily apparent. Can a home government stand aside and allow multinational firms on a large scale to enter into integrated production commitments with a variety of foreign governments? The active role of the U. S. government in the Automobile Pact, allocating production between Canada and the United States, is an indication of the way in which a home government may feel it must intervene to protect both jobs and balance-of-payments interests in such arrangements.

This line of reasoning suggested by the workshop participants speculated on a growing role of the home government in the activities of multinational firms. Comments by Olivier Giscard D'Estaings and Noritake Kobayashi indicated that the European and Japanese governments have already moved far in this direction. This prospect raises two further questions which are rather special to the U. S. situation, though they have some implications for other home governments. The first lies in the traditional pattern of government-business relations in the United States, characterized by limited contact and a tendency toward greater conflict than cooperation. The workshop participants foresaw considerable difficulty in establishing more effective working relationships. Some felt strongly that the U. S.

government should be excluded from the whole process, that its contributions were too small, compared to the adverse affects of its participation. But, the prognosis for the future suggests that both parties will have to find new ways, if there is to be a greater degree of interaction and particularly if there must be more cooperation in pursuit of a greater supporting role by the government.

The second and more difficult problem, spelled out by David Blake and Jerome Rosow, lies in the foreign-image implications of closer collaboration between U. S. government and business. The prevailing fear of neo-economic imperialism is already a heavy load for both U. S. business and government to carry within their relations overseas. As the arguments favoring greater intervention by the U. S. government grow, the negative aspects of increasing this image will be a significant deterrent. But, to the extent that they do prevail, it would appear that both parties will pay the price in some loss of effectiveness in their relations with host governments. Despite these deterrents, the discussion accepted implicitly a transition toward a greater U. S.-government role, for example, in the OPEC negotiations in the oil industry, and within the OECD efforts to improve investment conditions. In light of the major importance of the two deterrents noted, however, it is clear that the development of effective interaction between the U. S. government and the multinational firms will be a long and difficult process, and one to which considerable thought may be devoted usefully.

Among the home governments in Europe and Japan, there would not appear to be a major deterrent, such as those that apply to the United States, although there are some indications that the foreign policy implications of involvement with their multinational firms for the Japanese government in Southeast Asia may be somewhat similar to those of the United States. De. Kapoor pointed out a further problem for the Japanese in the higher expectations host countries in their area have for their behavior, because they are fellow Asians—expectations which may not be fulfilled by the Japanese. The relatively provincial, traditional Japanese outlook has not prepared them well for this role. However, by and large, the European and Japanese governments have already involved themselves more strongly in the affairs of their multinational firms. Unfortunately, the European experience in this regard has not been explored systematically, so the workshop provided little insight in its nature. The Japanese government has set forth explicit guidelines for its multinational firms, which Professor Kobayashi summarized. There are three main goals:

1) To serve the Japanese national interest;
2) To integrate with host-country national interest;
3) To relate to international regulations.

When expansion abroad is undertaken, it should be integrated with the total international Japanese structure in a cooperative manner, recognizing that the government will provide certain infrastructure elements of the system. Specific guidelines are designed to:

1) Encourage the development of local processing units;
2) Permit 50-50 joint ventures;
3) Develop local managerial resources;
4) Cooperate in local technological development;
5) Reinvest profits locally;
6) Do not disturb existing labor or commercial practices;
7) Do not overconcentrate in particular industries.

The Japanese government has set forth its concept quite explicitly. However, its operating experience under these guidelines is of brief duration, and it is not clear as to how they work out in practice. In noting some tendency for the firm to disassociate from government goals, Professor Kobayashi indicated the possibility of problems in this regard, but the evidence as yet is too slim. Studies of experience under this pattern are clearly indicated, therefore, as useful information for the guidance for other home governments.

THE GOVERNMENT-BUSINESS INTERFACE

The set of government and business goals outlined above could be readily combined in a three-dimensional matrix, from which a great variety of interface situations could be derived. This, indeed, is an accurate picture of the real world in which host and home governments and multinational firms find their paths crossing in a multitude of ways. It is impractical here to deal in any comprehensive way with these many facets of the international government-business interface. It is practical, however, to cut through this situational mass and deal with the subject in terms of a limited number of characteristics of the interface, which is the direction in which the workshop participants moved in their discussion.

The items in the discussion fell into two broad categories: visible or surface conflicts and the fundamental differences of approach underlying them. The surface issues range from the simple to the complex. They cover a multitude of subjects. In general, however, they tend to fall into two groups—economic and control. While the economic issues may involve a great deal of bargaining, they are susceptible to computation and to long- and short-term evaluations, which facilitate a cost-benefit analysis in which the interests of the parties may be reasonably balanced.

The control issues are more troublesome because a systematic analysis is more difficlult, and because they strike to the heart of vital aspects of the goals of both governments and multinational firms. For a national government, control within its domain is fundamental to the general concepts of sovereignty and the practical objectives of economic direction common to all modern governments. On the other hand, a degree of control by corporate headquarters is fundamental to the efficiency and fiscal responsibility of the multinational firm The ability to control transmission of skills and other resources is basic to competent performance of capital, production, and supplies on a global basis which in turn are essential to the efficiency of the global system—the hallmark of the multinational firm as a social institution.

The conflict of these goals is obvious. The more significant point, which was recognized in various ways in the workshop discussion, is the fact that any compromise between the two goals has a price which, to some degree, is paid by both parties. For example, Mr. Boothalingham remarked that he recognized that mixed ventures, which preserved a greater degree of control for the Indian government, probably involved a sacrifice of efficiency, which they accepted as the price for this greater degree of Indian control.

The more difficult issues of the interface, however, concern the fundamental implications of the visible conflicts and their resolution. Three aspects in particular were noted along this line during the workshop discussions. First, there is a simple question of degree of government involvement, in effect a questioning of how many issues should appear on the government-business interface and how many should be left to natural market processes. The participants did not explicitly explore this question. Between the lines of a large part of the discussion, however, one can readily read their feeling that more and more decisions will move from the marketplace to the government-business interface. Clearly, the implication of this is that the size and the complexity of the interface will grow. But, other than the traditional distress in the business community because of this development, there seemed little inclination to make an issue of it.

The second fundamental aspect is the volume of issues between a firm and a government, and the aggregate implications of the way those decisions are resolved. Eric Kierans expressed this problem by saying that he felt many specific decisions could be made in the direction desired by a foreign firm, with a satisfactory immediate outcome for the country. But, taken collectively, a number of those decisions could be quite adverse to the country. The significance of this observation is readily apparent in a country like Canada where 60 percent of the manufacturing is controlled by foreign firms. As Professor Kierans observed, the aggregate effect of a multitude of investment decisions is to distort substantially the opportunities open to the host government and its own nationals. The obvious implication of this point is that individual decisions must be made with reference to a larger national strategy, rather than on the basis of immediate considerations for a specific situation. This, however, has proved to be a very difficult process for host governments. A few, like Japan, seem to have been quite successful, though at the price of very strong governmental economic control. At the other extreme, Canada has had great difficulty arriving at anything approaching a consensus on even the broadest guidelines for handling foreign firms. At another extreme, one finds approaches, such as that adopted by the Andean group of countries, which are moving toward a strongly-stated broad policy which may prove counterproductive, when applied to individual cases.

A third underlying problem already has been suggested by the discussion of the difficulties and uncertainties of decisions pertaining to national goals by governments. There is a grave possibility that in many instances, in the present nationalistic mood, nation-oriented thinking will determine goals at the expense of true benefits to the people. Dr. Laserna spoke to this point when he observed that there is a tendency today to exert too much control because of preoccupation with economic goals for which it is apparently useful, but that this degree of control is destructive of other human desires. Also pertinent is Olivier Giscard d'Estaing's observation, noted earlier, about a multinational approach being needed because national governments are too preoccupied with nationally-oriented approaches to satisfactorily meet the needs of the people.

While these observations point to somewhat different directions, they both emphasize the basic characteristic of the modern national government, which is the central factor in this discussion. These governments are basically constrained in their thinking, in the influences to which they are subject and in the avenues of actions open to them by the boundaries of their nation; and the pressures of the times have heavily channeled their decisions along economic lines. This whole structure is strongly reinforced by attitudinal and emotional forces outlines in Chapter 2. As a result, it is extremely difficult for governments to arrive at decisions from a viewpoint which is broader either in spatial or in human dimensions. The multinational firm has a much more limited framework in a sense, but, in another sense, it is much broader because its spatial outlook is global and its constituency consists of individual human beings in an apolitical context. We enter here into a complex and probably controversial area of consideration of the social functions of governments and business firms. Without attempting to resolve those issues, it will suffice to identify, as the third major fundamental problem, the fact that the firm may, at least at times, be arguing more effectively for the interests of many individuals in a country than the government of that country, even though, as the debate appears on the government-business interface, the government claims to be doing precisely the opposite.

The workshop discussion did not give appreciable attention to one aspect of the international business-government interface, the conflicts between home and host governments in which the firm is a relatively powerless pawn. The conspicuous cases of this nature in recent years have involved intraterritorial application of U. S. antitrust and trading-with-the-enemy laws. The fact that this type of situation did not come up in the discussions indicates that despite the high visibility of the occasional case, this general type of problem does not figure importantly in the eyes of business or government. Looking down the road, however, we would suggest that it may be of increasing concern. The key issue, which has the potential for increasing its importance, is production allocation with its employment implications. For example, between Canada and the United States there is a stiffening of relations revolving around the efforts to foster U. S. employment through DISC and changes in the Automotive Agreement with the Burke-Hartke bill looming in the background, all of which Canadians believe will hurt their employment. The risk is that they will counter with other pressures to hold jobs, and the multinational firms will be caught between these conflicting government objectives. One can readily perceive similar conflicts involving other countries. Thus, though this subject is not currently pressing, it is one to which research may be fruitfully directed, in light of the prospective conflicts.

THE ACCOMMODATION PROCESS

While the elements of conflict in the government-business relationship were recognized, the basic thrust of the workshop discussion was in the direction of achievement of accommodation between the parties. In effect, the participants assumed throughout that the need was to identify the issues and to examine the ways in which they might be resolved. Most of the discussion concerned possible patterns of resolution, but there were some comments about the elements which contributed to the resolution which should be noted. Essentially, these fall under two headings: knowledge and power.

The knowledge aspect started with discussion by Richard Robinson early in the workshop, who stated that we need better environmental analysis to determine what the goals of governments are so that businesses could better relate their performance to them. This implies, in the first instance, a greater effort on the part of firms to learn what governments and countries are seeking. But as the discussions subsequently developed, a large part of the problem lies within the lack of definition of goals by countries, which has been discussed earlier in the chapter. On the other side of the coin, they found a need for government people to acquire greater understanding of the motivations and objectives of business firms. This subject is closely related to the external affairs activities discussed by Professor Boddewyn in his chapter.

The comments on power were brief but to the point, and because of these characteristics they seemed to take care of the subject quite adequately. Early in the discussion, one participant observed that the multinational firm has power because of the options available to it. Another retorted that power arose from the will of the people, expressed through the government. Virtually no more was said explicitly about this subject, but in the discussion in many ways it was made clear that the participants generally accepted the fact that it was the balance of power between these two concepts which determines the pattern of accommodation between the goals of firms and governments.

Related to this question of power were varied observations about the implications of increasing numbers of multinational firms from different countries upon the pattern of government-business relations. Mr. Boothalingham and Olivier Giscard d'Estaing expressed the view that the presence of a great number of firms in the area would strengthen the hand of host governments by permitting them many more options in their bargaining process. On the other hand, Professor Kierans was concerned lest the cumulative pressure of many multinational firms would add to the aggregate of their impact upon host countries, underscoring his point in the previous section about the difference between aggregate and individual decisions.

Most of the discussion of the accommodation process centered around the pattern of activities which might result from the interaction of government and business goals. Early in the first day, Professor Behrman observed that a "system of mutations" would evolve to satisfy the desires of host governments and this term stuck as the "buzz word" for subsequent discussion. It aptly described the general sense that the future lay in variations of forms and relationships to fit the varied environments to be expected.

Emphasizing the growth-survival goals mentioned earlier, Mr. Rosow and Mr. Thompson felt that multinational firms would prove to be highly adaptive in the future. Mr. Groo concurred, but did underscore the need for retention of enough control and power by the firm to give reality to survival. He emphasized the need for governments to recognize this limit.

The main thrust of all of the mutations proposed was in the direction of a more limited, less comprehensive role of the multinational firm, with a strengthening of the units within each country. It is not clear, however, whether this implies a major weakening of the role of the multinational firm in international economic decision-making and/or an attempt to retreat from an internationalized economy by individual nations to check the erosion of their economic sovereignty. Some comments by the participants suggested that the firm would continue to perform fully those internation functions in which it was effective, such as logistic planning and technological flows, the strengthening of local national units being limited to functions and industries for which international integration was of minor importance, whereas sensitivity to local interests was highly significant. The discussion along these lines in the workshop, however, was highly speculative, being labeled by one participant as "futurology." It seems clear, therefore, that considerable exploration of the forms of mutation which will be feasible and useful lies ahead.

Within this general concept, ideas of varied character were developed concerning ownership, integration, size, role, and risk.

The discussion of *ownership* was characteristic of the trend of current thinking, in striking contrast to that common just a few years ago. In the mid 1960s, and perhaps even later than that, such a discussion would have been largely preoccupied with pro and con arguments about joint ventures and varying degrees of local national ownership. There were some comments along this line, especially in its more sophisticated forms. Professors Kobayashi and Robinson discussed the frequent acceptance by Japanese firms of joint ventures, accompanied by contractual supply arrangements for export marketing. There was a brief discussion of the merits of local participation in ownership of stock in the parent corporation, which was advocated by Mr. Groo, but opposed by Professor Kierans as a drain on balance of payments of the host country. Professor Behrman observed that in some cases host governments might take an equity position in parent companies in order to gain access to information about their operations. Mr. Boothalingham mentioned, as noted previously, the merits of mixed ventures, while Olivier Giscard d'Estaing felt they would not survive long because the government would want a greater degree of control over them. However, he thought that it might be a very useful step in the early stage of development. All of these comments suggested that ownership patterns will be one of the main forms of mutation evolution in years to come. However, argumentation over the concept of shared ownership did not occupy the participants, perhaps because the concept has been generally accepted, as it was not a few years ago, but, perhaps more importantly, because its significance has waned.

The significant issue is now seen by perceptive men, like those in the workshop, to lie in *control*, not ownership. As Mr. Boothalingham observed, nations are strong and their methods are changing and varied ways will be found to control the firm. Dr. Laserna spoke of the advantage of separating the notion of property rights from that of control. From a "functional" point of view, i. e, one which enables a corporation to carry out its activities, the necessity is that of being able to control its operations and organization. The "right of property" is only one means of assuring such control. It is the same with land ownership for modern agricultural enterprises.

The Gray Report which had been released just before the workshop by the government of Canada takes a similar view. When compared to some earlier reports by government-sponsored groups which emphasized the ownership aspect, the Gray Report gives minor attention to the idea of repatriating ownership of foreign-owned firms. Rather, it places the major emphasis on measures which will directly assert control over them to achieve particular national goals.

It seems clear from this that, while there will undoubtedly be mutations in the ownership pattern in the future, more significant mutations will occur within the selective impairment of the control capabilities of the multinational firms. Following Mario Laserna's analysis, one may think of the traditional firm in a free society as controlling a "bundle of rights," including property rights, rights to location of production facilities, rights to the sale of a range of products, rights to advertise their characteristics, rights to acquire and allocate capital funds, etc. Even in domestic business, it has been true that individual rights have been constricted by governments without basically infringing the overall character or the underlying concept of property rights. It is, therefore, quite natural that in the international scene the same pattern should be pursued to achieve the particular desires of host and home governments. In fact, in retrospect, it seems strange that the preoccupation with ownership should have been so great. Upon careful examination, doubtless it will be found that that preoccupation had more to do with the symbolic meaning of ownership (perhaps related to implications of colonialism, imperialism, and nationalism) than to the realities of achieving the specific goals of governments.

The concept of *integration* stemmed mainly from Jack Behrman's proposals, which are outlined fully in his chapter. They rest, in large measure, on the desire of governments to achieve reasonable degrees of economic efficiency in the sharing of facilities, while retaining reasonable control. The participants recognized the institutional difficulties inherent in moving in this direction, particularly the difficulty of achieving intergovernment agreements which have hobbled such efforts as the Latin American Free Trade Area complementation-agreement program. Nonetheless, there was a feeling that this was a sound direction in which to move, given the objectives of both firms and governments, and that progress in that direction should be expected.

The question of *size* was most strongly expressed by Dr. Robinson. He felt that countries are concerned with the increasing size of firms, which represent a threat to their political status. He was doubtful that any form of international control will emerge to manage the firms on a political basis. He felt, therefore, that there would be strong pressure for limitations on the size of firms, and that this would result in the spin-off of foreign units and evolution of multinational networks of associated firms tied together by contractual relationships. Dr. Robinson observed that the Japanese multinational firms have been evolving this sort of associational model which may demonstrate its potentials. Professor Kobayashi cast some doubt on this point, however, stating that the system was forced upon the firms by government pressures, but that they did not basically accept it. This idea was not pursued further in the discussion. It would appear to be a feasible form of mutation, particularly in industries in which the rationale for tight global integration is limited; that is, industries in which skill flows from parent to subsidiary are small because technology is in a period of slow development, or where logistic integration is either limited or not complex. Household appliances, food products, and some other fields would fall under these categories. On the other hand, the computer and automobile industries would not seem so readily susceptible to this type of mutation.

The fourth approach was developed by Dr. Behrman, and took a rather different direction. He attempted to identify the *role* which host governments would assign to multinational firms in two types of countries, according to their special capabilities. In the developed countries, he felt the emphasis would be on industries where global capabilities were most significant, where cross-border capabilities had a special role (for example, cleaning up the Rhine River), and where high technology was important. In the less developed countries, he felt that national orientation would dominate. In those industries where technology was mature, he anticipated an expansion of the fade-out ownership concept already established in the Andean countries. He foresaw some role where systems analysis was useful—for example, in dealing with levels of unemployment in urban areas. He did expect some emphasis on the international capabilities of firms in situations where complementation arrangements were useful in Latin American and elsewhere and also where it was important to utilize the international capabilities of the firm for export marketing purposes. The firms provide, at present, the most practical means in many industries for host nations to integrate themselves within the international economy.

The discussion of *risk* centered around a proposal advanced by Richard Robinson. He suggested that the costs of political risk in host countries should be "socialized" to benefit both the countries and the firms. Currently, the high political risk results either in lack of investment or high profit requirements, representing both costs to the host country and a deterrent to realization of opportunities by firms. Dr. Robinson proposed a contractual relation between the country and firm, in which the former would underwrite the cost of the political risk, while the latter agreed to conditions satisfactorily serving national interests. He distributed the following draft:[1]

1) Strict political neutrality on the part of foreign-controlled and/or owned enterprises, foreign personnel, and contractors in host countries. A failure to maintain such neutrality would void all parent government political-risk guarantees that may be offered.

   Political neutrality might be defined as nonintervention in partisan politics except as a corporation might attempt to influence policies by means of *public* statements. Any *covert* activity of a political nature could be deemed a per se violation of neutrality.
2) Adherence to all local laws on the part of foreign-owned and/or controlled enterprises and contractors. Failure to do so should be a bar to any parent government pressure or intervention in event of expropriation or unilateral breach of contract by the host government, even without effective, prompt, and adequate compensation (unless the law be discriminating or of an ex post facto nature, i. e., a host nation violation of agreed-upon entry conditions).
3) A host government commitment to recognize foreign ownership of tangible and intangible rights, and/or management control of same, for twenty years (unless a shorter period is agreed upon at the time of entry). These rights should be inalienable during such period, if (1) the rights are established locally in accord with local law and upon the consent of an independent government, which is recognized internationally, and (2) the foreign investor and/or contractor adheres to the entry conditions unless adherence is made impossible either by the host government or by a change of circumstances beyond the control of the foreign interest involved.
4) Adherence by all signatory nations to the tax-sparing principle, so as to give full force to tax incentives and holidays, introduced by other members to foreign business interests.
5) The taxation by parent governments of flows of earnings arising under management, training, technical assistance, license agreements, and contracts at a capital gains rate, or at not more than fifty percent of the usual tax rate, whichever is less.
6) Agreement to refer disputes in respect to the interpretation of the rules to an international forum, to be created under the convention.

The subsequent discussion focused on certain critical questions concerning the feasibility of the scheme, including the important uncertainty as to the long-term strength of government assurances within the politics of countries for which the risks central to the scheme are important. But, the participants did feel the general concept of absorption of the cost of risks by the countries was sound, and that firms would be prepared to make some degree of commitment to reduce animosity and consequent uncertainty of investment.

MANAGEMENT AT THE INTERFACE

The final broad area covered in the workshop discussion was the stance adopted by multinational firms in relation to host governments, and the manner in which the firms' objectives were conveyed to the government. Professor Boddewyn provided the initial framework for this discussion along the lines presented in his chapter with a three-way breakdown of the means by which a firm related itself to the environment: first, making optimum effective use of the opportunities offered by the environment; second, assuring legitimacy for continuing operation within the environment; and, third, attempts to make the environment move in a favorable direction. The first point, which pertains to such matters as making use of tax incentives offered by the government or relating effectively to government service organizations, involves no difficult questions which concerned the workshop participants. Companies are generally quite conscious of the merits of this type of activity, even though their effectiveness in it may vary considerably.

The need to establish the legitimacy of their operations in host countries is also, by now, quite well recognized among multinational managements. But, the manner in which this goal is pursued, and the handling of the third objective, i. e., influencing the environment, still pose many questions which the participants explored. Henry Thompson expressed one philosophy of those who regard these matters as critical tasks in relating to host governments. The point of view in communications with the government, he said, should be one of trying to determine whether there is a place in the host society in which the firm can make a contribution, and how it should go about making that contribution. The continuing objective should be to build up a sense of confidence and assurance with the government that the behavior of the firm is in line with the government's goals. He believed that it was quite possible that firms would have an impact on government policy, but that they should take no initiative in presenting their views for this purpose. Their stance should rather be a passive one, waiting for the government to come to them seeking advice. He felt that this sort of policy was the most likely to have a real impact.

Todd Groo presented a philosophy which is consistent with that of Henry Thompson, but went slightly past it in suggesting the degree of company initiative required. He characterized the objective as one of attempting to keep an open and sympathetic market within which the company could function effectively. There is a need within this goal to try to avert government decisions which might work against the requirements of effective operation. He did not feel it was wise to engage in ideological discussions, but he did feel that, in many cases, adverse government decisions were the consequence of lack of sufficient knowledge in order to properly gauge the consequences of policy changes. Thus, he felt it was sound for the firm to take the initiative in communicating information to the government, so that the full implications of policy alternatives would be clear. This sort of stance, he felt, could result, in some degree, in moving government policy in directions which were favorable to the operations of the firm.

Professor Crozier indicated the potentiality of still greater initiative by referring to the reforms a few years ago in Le Patronat (CNPF), the French capstone business organization. Le Patronat had been a very passive, conservative organization for many years. A few years ago, it substantially liberalized its outlook, and took initiatives which resulted in some important influences upon French government policy. One of the key members of the liberalizing group was the president of the French Shell organization. He generalized from this opinion to the view that executives in foreign firms can play a strong role in the evolution of host-government policy.

Concurrence with this general philosophy was expressed by Jerome Rosow. He felt that it was basically sound for multinational firms to attempt to influence the general policy of host countries. The only major reservation in his opinion was that firms should avoid any involvement in the political party system. His company vigorously adheres to an apolitical stance in host societies, but otherwise enters actively into discussions of policies with the government. Mr. Groo advocated a policy which represents something of a middle ground between that of Mr. Rosow and the potential described by Professor Crozier. He felt that the firm itself should avoid involvement in the evolution of host-government policies but that individual executives in each country should be free to act and individually judge what was appropriate.

At this point Professor Blake interjected the objection that giving a high degree of latitude to local executives on such important matters was apparently in conflict with the concept of a rationalized integrated firm. Professor Kierans provided substance for this comment by describing the situation in Canada. The national manufacturing association there is influenced heavily by the viewpoints of senior executives of multinational subsidiaries because of the very large component of foreign business in Canadian society. On the important national issue of trade policy, these people tend to favor protectionism because they have a personal vested interest in it. A more liberal trade policy might result in weakening the position of a number of subsidiaries whose factories were set up in large part to be free of Canadian tariff barriers. The viewpoints of these officers, however, are not necessarily in line with either the interest of Canada or with the basic policies of their parent firms, the latter presumably preferring to move toward more liberalized trade policies around the world. In such circumstances, therefore, it was clearly questionable whether local executives could have free rein to influence host government policy according to their own inclinations.

Further viewpoints of this line of thought developed from discussion of the experience of the Council of the Americas and its predecessor organizations in Latin America. An early prime goal of this organization was the promotion of the private-enterprise system in Latin America, in the expectation that this would improve the image of multinational firms and result in government policies favorable to private enterprise. The results were not effective, and some participants deduced from this and related experiences that it was basically unsound for multinational firms to attempt to influence host societies at a broad policy or ideological level. An opposing viewpoint expressed, however, was that this was a pragmatic matter, to be judged according to the practical aspects of the situation. Efforts with an ideological thrust were quite appropriate if there were chances of some success, as compared to the Latin American environment in which hostility to expanded appreciation of private enterprise is so great.

The outcome of the Council of the Americas' activities was presented as suggestive of the selective approach to influencing the environment, which is evolving as businessmen become more sophisticated in this area. Its main thrust at present is by means of a quiet campaign of communication with elites to define ways in which firms may work effectively with countries. On the surface, this apparently falls primarily under the legitimacy heading. However, the indirect strengthening of influence with the elites may well contribute to general policy evolution, with the permissive frame of mind Henry Thompson's approach suggested. This is probably the method which will be both feasible and effective in the Latin American context. The sense of the discussion among the participants, however, was clear: very different goals and approaches would be practical and feasible as businesses moved from country to country.

Interwoven in this discussion of the stance of multinational firms were a variety of comments about the means by which their views were communicated to host governments. Some elements of this aspect have already been noted in the question of the role of the individual executive of a subsidiary versus that of his corporation, and of general associations such as the Council of the Americas. The general tenor of the discussion suggested quite varied viewpoints and substantial uncertainty as to the role of various communication media, suggesting that this area required considerable further research.

At one end of the spectrum, Mr. Thompson felt that more and more firms would be stating their viewpoints in collaborative partnership with local joint-venture associates. At the other end of the spectrum, there was some support for broad organizational efforts. Mr. Groo, for example, while noting that he felt a corporation had to perform the communication function itself, for the most part did support groups like the Atlantic Institute and the Council of the Americas. He felt that relatively objective groups of this nature were working in a sound direction, and that it was appropriate for firms to support their programs.

Somewhere between these poles were more limited associational efforts to achieve objectives which, depending upon the circumstances in any particular country, were considered effective. For example, Dr. Boddewyn noted the growing corporativism in Europe, and his expectation that associations would have increasing legitimacy in exerting influence on government policy, with the implicit assumption that U. S. firms should be utilizing them to a greater degree. However, for the immediate future, the consensus among the business participants seemed to be that their utility was limited. Todd Groo, for example, felt that American chambers of commerce abroad were primarily helpful as sources of information and learning techniques for local executives who wanted to keep in touch with other businessmen. Henry Thompson noted that organizations were often useful in pushing certain ideas in a testing-exploratory way, when individual firms or executives felt it was premature to advocate them individually.

While the limited depth to which views along this line were explored was partly a function of the time available in the workshop, it was also apparent that this is an area in which corporate experience is still in an early stage and, as suggested in Dr. Boddewyn's paper, much still needs to be learned about what is effective.

To this point we have focused on one side of management at the interface, efforts by the multinational firm to gain legitimacy and convey its viewpoints to governments. This focus appeared in our notes on the discussion because that aspect was covered in a particular block of time in the workshop. However, the other side of the subject—government influences upon the firm—did, in fact, receive as much or more attention diffused throughout the two-day period. It would be redundant to devote much space to it here, because comments along that line run throughout the earlier parts of this chapter. It will suffice at this point, therefore, to note a few key points.

The fact that governments have exerted effective influence is readily evident in the change in actions of multinational firms—the structural mutations and related operational characteristics. The methods by which influence has been exerted are varied, but the major element evident in the workshop discussions is the investment-entry process. Dr. Robinson's chapter provides an elaboration of its role. It seems clear that there is growing sophistication in the terms which governments present and the skill with which they negotiate new investment agreements. Lying behind this process, of course, are basic policy guidelines as to ownership, technology, exports, and other aspects of operations. While further evolution in this direction is certainly to be expected, aided by research such as Dr. Robinson suggests, we can conclude that in this area governments have developed highly effective means for influencing multinational firms.

Beyond the entry process, however, lies a vast area of ongoing operational activities and policies over which governments try to exert influence, but for which interaction processes are less defined and developed. A major complication in discussing them is that they blend in with domestic government-business relstions, e. g., what is the difference between persuading a multinational firm to do more exporting and pushing a domestic firm in the same direction? There are differences, but also similarities, so the influence processes are not so neatly defined as in the entry stage. Another complication is that the definition of bargaining power and options is much fuzzier than in the entry negotiations. One may say that the power balance has shifted markedly toward the government once an investment is in place because the firm cannot simply withhold its capital and technology. But the firm retains substantial strength in its management of technology flows, its global servicing capabilities, and other assets useful to the nation. Finally, there is the sheer administrative task for a government of monitoring in any great detail the operations of firms as a basis for exerting influence.

The workshop discussion provided little insight into the evolution of this aspect of the government-influence process. There were implications in the emphasis on control vs. ownership that governments would be moving toward influencing firms in selected aspects of operations. But the mechanisms by which influence would be exerted are varied and have not been examined systematically, pointing to another significant area of future research.

SUMMARY

Perhaps the most effective summary of the workshop discussion was an observation by Mr. Groo to the effect that, instead of hearing radical proposals for change, virtually all that had been said added up to continued evolution of the multinational firm and its relations with governments in directions which were already in process. Realistically, this is the way the world has usually progressed. There have been some traumatic, sharp breaks in the history of international business-government affairs, starting most conspicuously with the Mexican expropriations of oil properties. But, by and large, the history has, as in most things, been one of evolution.

The discussion of goals of governments and firms, and the process of their accommodation, was useful, therefore, primarily in identifying the thinking and actions at the leading edge of the evolutionary process. Perhaps the greatest progress in the last decade or so has been made in defining the goals of the firms and, to a greater degree, of the countries whose interests are so complex and varied, and in the education of each party of the goals of the other. Compared to the rather simplistic confrontations of the early sixties, we now have more knowledgeable people working on both sides of the interface, at least in the most sophisticated situations. Still, it was clear from the discussion that a great deal more progress is needed in this direction, particularly among the governments who have a difficult problem in defining their interests intellectually, and in working out the priorities among them through the ever-difficult political processes of democratic society. Until these goals are better defined, there will, inevitably, be substantial complication of the accommodation process, due to ignorance and to changes attributable to the steady reduction of ignorance, and consequent shifts in priorities related to that reduction.

The other major change, in recent years, has been the evolution toward conception, and acceptance of varied mutations of relations between governments and multinational firms. As compared again to rather simplistic concepts revolving largely around sharply defined opinions of degrees of ownership-sharing in the early sixties, we have now not only much more flexible views about ownership on the part of firms, but, more importantly, a more flexible and perceptive view on the part of government as to the distinction between ownership and control. Furthermore,there is at least a beginning of development of arrangements, such as the integration of production among countries, which look toward the day when the global capabilities of the international firm are used to serve the people of the world effectively, rather than acting as a source of frustration, in conflict with the restricted nation-oriented outlook of governments. But the present developments are just a small beginning in this direction, and they clearly indicate that the major challenges for the future lie in developing new mutations and perfecting their application.

Notes

Chapter Two
Attitudes Affecting International Business-Government Affairs

1. Jack N. Behrman, *National Interests and the Multinational Enterprise* (Englewood Cliffs, N. J.: Prentice-Hall, 1970), p. 31; Raymond F. Mikesell et al., *Foreign Investment in the Petroleum and Mineral Industries* (Baltimore, Md.: Johns Hopkins, 1971), p. 29; and Raymond Vernon, *Sovereignty at Bay* (New York: Basic Books, 1971), pp. 192-230.

2. Vernon, op. cit., p. 230.

3. Behrman, op. cit., pp. 32-87.

4. John Fayerweather, "Attitudes of British, Canadian, and French Elites toward Foreign Companies," *International Studies Quarterly,* December 1972: "Variables Influencing Elite Attitudes toward Foreign Firms," Working paper 72-42 (mimeographed), Graduate School of Business Administration, New York University 1972; and Claude McMillan, Jr. et al., *International Enterprise in a Developing Economy* (East Lansing: Graduate School of Business Administration, Michigan State University, 1964), p. 45.

5. Fayerweather, "Attitudes" and working paper, op. cit.

6. Jack N. Behrman, op. cit. pp. 55-69.

7. John Fayerweather, "Nationalism and the Multinational Firm," *The Multinational Enterprise in Transition,* eds. Ashok Kapoor and Phillip D. Grub (Princeton: Darwin, 1972).

8. Vernon, op. cit., pp. 193-201.

9. Kari Levitt, *Silent Surrender* (New York: St. Martin's Press, 1970).

10. John Delamater, Daniel Katz, and Herbert C. Kelman, "On the Nature of National Involvement: A Preliminary Study." *The Journal of Conflict Resolution,* September 1969, pp. 320-357.

11. Fayerweather, "Attitudes," op. cit.

12. Fayerweather, working paper, op. cit.

13. I. A. Litvak and C. J. Maule, *Foreign Investment: The Experience of Host Countries* (New York: Praeger, 1970), pp. 3-30; L. C. Nehrt, *The Political Climate of Foreign Investment* (New York: Praeger, 1970); F. R. Root, "U. S. Business Abroad and Political Risks," *MSU Business Topics,* Winter 1968, pp. 73-80; and S. H. Robock, "Political Risk: Identification and Assessment," *Columbia Journal of World Business,* July-August 1971, pp. 6-20.

14. J. Alex Murray, "Guidelines for U. S. Investment in Canada," *Columbia Journal of World Business,* May-June 1971, pp. 29-37.

15. Fayerweather,"Attitudes," op. cit.

16. I. A. Litvak, C. R. Maule, and R. D. Robinson, *Dual Loyalty* (Toronto: McGraw-Hill, 1971).

17. Ashok Kapoor, *International Business Negotiations* (New York: New York University Press, 1970), pp. 279-281.

18. John Fayerweather, *The Mercantile Bank Affair* (White Plains, N. Y.: International Arts & Sciences Press, 1973) and Ashok Kapoor, op. cit.

19. R. A. Bauer, I. de Sola Pool, and L. A. Dexter, *American Business and Public Policy* (New York: Atherton Press, 1963).

20. Jack N. Behrman, *Multinational Production Consortia* (Washington: Government Printing Office, 1971).

Chapter Three
Beyond the Multinational Corporation

1. In the characteristic international firm, interest and expertise relating to exploitation of foreign markets tends to be limited to an international division, but with functional expertise remaining in the domestic divisions and domestically-oriented staff departments. Decisions are less biased than in a *foreign-oriented* firm, structurally characterized by a staff foreign or export department, in terms of the type of foreign market-entry strategy that will be considered, but are still heavily biased nationally. Highly centralized control is maintained, and key positions overseas are filled with home-country nationals. In the *multinational firm,* international interest and expertise tend to be spread throughout the firm.

2. A number of non-U. S. nationals are now appearing in top executive positions with U. S. corporate headquarters—for example, 900 out of the 2000-man IBM World Trade Corporation Headquarters in New York, including a president of French origin. Unfortunately, this critical subject has not been adequately researched, so one can project no figures. A study based on 1965 data reported less than one percent of the executives in 150 New York-based internationally-active firms were non-U. S. nationals. (Kenneth Simmonds, "Multinational? Well Not Quite," *Columbia Journal of World Business,* Fall 1966, pp. 115-122). The situation may have changed significantly since then, particularly in regard to European regional headquarters personnel. Also, U. S. entry barriers for foreign executives have been relaxed. It may be

revealing that a survey of 1,029 directors, conducted in the course of the Harvard study of multinational corporations, turned up only 19 foreigners, of whom 14 were either Canadian or British. (Vernon, op. cit., *Sovereignty at Bay,* (New York: Basic Books, 1971), p. 146).

3. Vernon, op. cit., p. 145. One problem is, of course, the definition of multinational. See p. 15n.5. Also, there is considerable difficulty in tracing ownership. Finally, the Harvard data is perhaps five years out of date.

4. Howard Perlmutter, "Geocentric Giants to Rule Business World," *Business Abroad,* April 1969, p. 9.

Chapter Four
Can the Multinational Enterprise Gain Acceptability through Industrial Integration?

1. John Elac and Jaime Undurraga, *La Empresa Industrial en la Integración de América Latina* (Buenos Aires: INTAL, December 1971).

2. A fourth exists within the provincial governments or a nation; their attitudes toward the MNE differ considerably from those in the other three, and may sometimes be the dominant ones.

3. Elac and Undurraga, op. cit.

4. I have detailed this proposal in "Sharing, International Production," *Law and Policy in International Business,* Spring 1972, p. 1.

Chapter Five
The Engagement of Host Government Interests upon the Entry of Foreign Business

1. Prida Hetrakul, *The Promotion of Direct Foreign Investment in Thailand* (Cambridge: Alfred P. Sloan School of Management, Massachusetts Institute of Technology, unpublished MS thesis, 1970), summarized from Chapter 6.

2. *International Financial News Survey,* vol. 24, no. 7, February 23, 1972, p. 52.

3. G. B. Meeker, *The Feasibility of the Fade-Out Joint Venture Principle as a Form of Direct U. S. Private Investment in Latin America* (Washington, D. C.: Georgetown University, unpublished MBA thesis, 1970). (Summarized in Guy B. Meeker, "Fade-out Joint Venture: Can it Work for Latin America? " in *Inter-America Economic Affairs,* Spring 1971), p. 25.

4. Ibid., p. 58.

5. Ibid., p. 59.

6. Ibid., pp. 62-63.

7. Philippe Bouckaert, Paul Christenson, William Cowan, Jesus Dualan, Alfred Duncan, E. Taylor Harmon, Sudhir Kilachand, Marcelo Leon,

John Nunley, Thomas Ronai, Dirck Schou, Eric Spector, Joseph Tischler, Ahmed Yehia; Faculty Advisor, and Vis. Prof. Charles H. Savage, Jr. Reported in "How Will Multinational Firms React to the Andean Pact's Decision 24?",*Inter-American Economic Affairs,* Autumn 1971, p. 55.

8. Ibid., p. 64.

Chapter Six The External Affairs Function in American Multinational Corporations

1. Harmon Zeigler, *Interest Groups In American Society* (Englewood Cliffs, N. J.: Prentice Hall, 1964); and R. A. Bauer et al., *American Business and Public Policy: The Politics of Foreign Trade* (New York: Atherton Press, 1963). There is also a "scandal" literature on influence peddling in high places, as well as historical studies of business-government relations in America. Marxist and neo-Marxist economists equally have been concerned with the interface between business and its publics.

2. "Organization and Environment," *International Studies of Management and Organization,* Fall 1972.

3. Ashok Kapoor, *International Business Negotiations: A Study in India* (New York University Press, 1970); and John Fayerweather, *The Mercantile Bank Affair* (White Plains, N. Y.: International Arts & Sciences Press, 1973).

4. Geoffrey Kean, *The Public Relations Man Abroad* (New York: Praeger, 1968).

5. Jack Behrman, *Some Patterns in the Rise of the Multinational Enterprise* (Chapel Hill, N. C.: Graduate School of Business, University of North Carolina, 1969), pp. 115-18; *National Interests and the Multinational Enterprise* (Englewood Cliffs, N. J.: Prentice-Hall, 1970); *U. S. International Business and Governments* (New York: McGraw-Hill, 1971); and Ashok Kapoor, "Business-Government Relations Become Respectable." *Columbia Journal of World Business* (July-August 1970).

6. David Burtis et al., *Multinational Corporation Nation-State Interaction; An Annotated Bibliography* (Philadelphia: Foreign Policy Research Institute, 1971). Several doctoral dissertations at New York University's Graduate School of Business Administration are also relevant: I. T. Tan, "Business-Government Relations in Southeast Asia: Study of Singapore and Malaysia" (1972); C. N. Aguilar, "External Affairs at the World Headquarters Level of the U. S. Based Multinational Enterprise" (in process); and R. L. Torneden, "Foreign Disinvestment by U. S. Multinational Corporations: A Preliminary Study" (in process).

7. A. Kapoor and J. Boddewyn, *International Business-Government Relations; U. S. Corporate Experience in Asia and Western Europe* (New York: American Management Association, 1973).

8. There is extensive and excellent literature to that effect by

such scholars as Raymond Vernon, Richard D. Robinson, Jack N. Behrman, John Fayerweather, and Charles P. Kindleberger. See also: J. Boddewyn, "Issues Between the Multinational Corporation and Host Governments: The European Case," Ashok Kapoor and Phillip D. Grub, eds., *The Multinational Enterprise in Transition* (Princeton, N. J.: Darwin Press, 1972).

9. For a more detailed analysis of these factors, see: J. Boddewyn and A. Kapoor, "The External Relations of American Multinational Enterprises," *International Studies Quarterly* (December 1972).

10. For discussions to that effect, see J. Boddewyn, "Don't Take Belgium for Granted," *Worldwide P & I Planning* (November-December 1969), 39-49; and Ashok Kapoor, "Business-Government Relations Become Respectable," *Columbia Journal of World Business* (July-August 1970), pp. 27-32.

Chapter Seven
Government, Politics, and the Multinational Enterprise

1. National Industrial Conference Board, *Obstacles and Incentives to Private Foreign Investment, 1967-1968,* vol. I: *Obstacles* (New York: National Industrial Conference Board, 1969), p. 2.

2. This section on influence has been stimulated by Neil A. McDonald, *Politics: A Study of Control Behavior* (New Brunswick, N. J.: Rutgers University Press, 1965) and James N. Rosenau, *Calculated Control as a Unifying Concept in the Study of International Politics and Foreign Policy* (Princeton, N. J.: Center of International Studies, 1963).

3. There are a number of excellent books on this topic, especially the following: Jack Behrman, *National Interests and the Multinational Enterprise: Tensions among the North Atlantic Countries* (Englewood Cliffs, N. J.: Prentice-Hall, 1970), John Fayerweather, *International Business Management: A Conceptual Framework* (New York: McGraw-Hill, 1969), Richard Robinson, *International Business Policy* (New York: Holt, Rinehart and Winston, 1964), and Raymond Vernon, *Sovereignty at Bay* (New York: Basic Books, 1971).

4. John Fayerweather, "Attitudes of British and French Elite Groups toward Foreign Companies," *MSU Business Topics,* Vol. XX (Winter, 1972), pp. 13-24.

5. For a further discussion of this and other related matters see, Jack Behrman, *U. S. International Business and Governments* (New York: McGraw-Hill, 1971).

6. The structural-functional approach followed here is most well-developed in Gabriel A. Almond and G. Bingham Powell, Jr., *Comparative Politics: A Development Approach* (Boston: Little, Brown & Co., 1966).

7. Ibid., p. 47.

8. Howard Perlmutter, "The Tortuous Evolution of the Multinational Corporation," *Columbia Journal of World Business* (January-February 1969), pp. 9-18.

Chapter Eight
The Negotiation Era and the Multinational Enterprise

1. For several articles relating to this point see A. Kapoor and Phillip D. Grub (eds.), *The Multinational Enterprise in Transition: Selected Readings and Essays* (Princeton, N.J.: Darwin Press, 1972).

2. This characteristic is becoming increasingly important in Asian countries. For additional comments see A. Kapoor and J. Boddewyn, *International Business-Government Relations: U.S. Corporate Experience in Asia and Western Europe* (American Management Association, 1973).

3. Fred C. Ikle, *How Nations Negotiate* (New York: Praeger, 1967), p. 2.

4. Thomas C. Schelling, *The Strategy of Conflict* (New York: Oxford University Press, 1960), p. 15.

5. *Ibid.,* p. 16.

6. Ikle, op. cit., p. 6.

7. Simon Williams, "Negotiating Investments in Emerging Countries," *Harvard Business Review,* January-February 1965, pp. 89-99.

8. For brief comments on the Bokaro steel project, see A. Kapoor, *International Business Negotiations: A Study in India* (New York University Press, 1970); Richard D. Robinson, *Cases in International Business* (New York: Holt, Rinehart & Winston, 1962) for a study of negotiations between Merck and the Indian government but with the constant awareness of the USSR's counter offers.

9. In principle, the same problem will exist for dominant investors from other countries, such as the Japanese in South East Asia.

10. This aspect was demonstrated in a recent visit to several Asian countries where host government officials and indigenous businessmen expressed keen interest to learn about the Andean foreign investment code.

11. Some of the Asian countries where this has occurred are South Korea, Indonesia, Singapore, India, Malaysia, and, to a lesser extent, the Philippines.

12. An in-depth study of the negotiation process within and between the MNE and HG is A. Kapoor's, *International Business Negotiations* , op. cit. Another study is by John Fayerweather on the Mercantile Bank Affair in Canada. Most of the literature relating to the general subject of negotiations is included in the bibliography in Kapoor's book.

13. The author is currently engaged in research along these lines, and the general range and variety of cases to be included has been generally defined.

14. A. Kapoor's *International Business Negotiations* is an example of a project which did not materialize.

Chapter Nine
Perspectives for the Future

1. This proposal has subsequently been published in Richard D. Robinson, "The Developing Countries, Development, and the Multinational Corporation,", *The Annals,* September, 1972, p. 78.

About the Authors

Jack N. Behrman, North Carolina University. Dr. Behrman has a B. S. from Davidson College, an M. A. from the University of North Carolina, and a Ph.D. from Princeton University. In 1945-46 he was with the International LaborOrganization. From 1946 to 1961 he served on the faculties of Davidson College, Princeton University, Washington and Lee University, and the University of Delaware. He was Deputy Assistant Secretary of Commerce and Assistant Secretary from 1961 to 1964. His publications include *Some Patterns in the Rise of the Multinational Enterprise, U. S. International Business and Governments,* and *National Interests and the Multinational Enterprise.*

David H. Blake, University of Pittsburgh. Dr. Blake has an A. B. from Dartmouth, an M.B.A. from the University of Pittsburgh, and Ph.D. from Rutgers University. He served on the faculty of Wayne State University from 1966 to 1969. His teaching and research is divided between political science and business. He edited the special issue of the *Annals* of the Academy of Political Science, devoted to the Multinational Firm (September, 1972).

J. Boddewyn, Baruch College. Dr. Boddewyn received the degrees of Commercial Engineer from the University of Louvain, M.B.A. from the University of Oregon, and D.B.A. from the University of Washington. He was on the faculties of the University of Portland from 1957 to 1964 and New York University from 1964 to 1973, joining Baruch in 1973. He served on the faculty of Centre d'Echanges Technologiques Internationaux in 1968. His publications include *Comparative Management and Marketing, World Business Systems* (editor and contributor), *International Business-Government Relations* (coauthor, to be published in 1973) and *Belgian Public Policy Toward Retailing.* He is editor of *International Studies of Management and Organization.*

John Fayerweather, New York University. Dr. Fayerweather has a B.S. in Geological Engineering from Princeton, and an M.B.A. and D.C.S. from Harvard. He served in England, France, and Korea during World War II. He was a member of the business school faculties of Harvard (1948-58) and Columbia (1958-60) before joining NYU. His books include *The Executive Overseas, International Business Management, Foreign Investment in Canada: Prospects for National Policy,* and *The Mercantile Bank Affair.* He is editor of *The International Executive.*

Ashok Kapoor, New York University. Dr. Kapoor received his bachelor's degree from Delhi University, and his M.B.A. and Ph.D. from North Carolina. He has been on the New York University faculty since 1966. His publications include *International Business Negotiations, Managing International Markets* (coauthor), *International Business-Government Relations* (coauthor, to be published in 1973), and *The Multinational Firm in Transition* (coeditor). He is a member of the executive committee of the Asia Society, and active in other international organizations. He works with the World Bank on simulated international business negotiations.

J. Alex Murray, University of Windsor. Professor Murray obtained his M.B.A. from McMaster University, and his doctorate from the University of Illinois. He has been associated with the Universities of Illinois, Michigan and Windsor, and has been a visiting professor at the Banff School of Management. His research and writings have been in the areas of Canadian-United States trade liberalization, international intelligence systems and attitudinal studies of foreign investment in Canada. He is presently director of the Seminar on Canadian-American Relations at the University of Windsor.

Richard D. Robinson, Massachusetts Institute of Technology and Harvard University. Dr. Robinson received his B.A. from the University of Washington, M.B.A. from Harvard, and Ph.D. from Massachusetts Institute of Technology. He served with the U. S. Army political intelligence in Korea. From 1947 to 1956 he was in Turkey, engaged primarily in research for the Institute of Current World Affairs and American Universities Field Staff, with special assignments for the World Bank, Ford Foundation, and U. S. government. In 1956 he joined the Harvard Business School faculty. Since 1962 he has divided his time between the Harvard Department of History and MIT. He is the author of several books, including *The First Turkish Republic, International Business Policy,* and *International Business Management,* and coauthor of *Dual Loyalty.*